ALCUIN CLUB COLLECTIONS
NO. XXVIII

STUDIES IN
EARLY ROMAN LITURGY

I. THE KALENDAR

BY

WALTER HOWARD FRERE, C.R.
D.D., Hon. Litt.D. (Leeds)
Bishop of Truro

OXFORD UNIVERSITY PRESS
LONDON: HUMPHREY MILFORD
1930

OXFORD UNIVERSITY PRESS
AMEN HOUSE, E.C. 4
LONDON EDINBURGH GLASGOW
LEIPZIG NEW YORK TORONTO
MELBOURNE CAPETOWN BOMBAY
CALCUTTA MADRAS SHANGHAI
HUMPHREY MILFORD
PUBLISHER TO THE
UNIVERSITY

Printed in Great Britain

PREFACE

THE Kalendar of the Roman Church lies at the roots of the development of the Kalendar in almost all the historic churches of the West. It is fitting therefore that a Study of Early Roman Liturgy should begin with this topic.

This essay has been rewritten several times at intervals during the last five years. The appearance of fresh evidence in manuscript or in print has necessitated such revision. It cannot be supposed that any final stage is reached now, for fresh documents may be found or be newly accessible which will fill up the many gaps and make deductions safer than they are at present. But I have felt that a point has been reached at which much that has been slowly garnered may well be utilized; and at which some generally accepted views, especially about Sacramentaries, need to be challenged.

It is in the first Part of this Essay, where the available evidence about the Kalendar is critically examined, that novel views are set out. In the second Part, the results thus acquired are brought to the investigation of the history and claims of the several entries in the Kalendar, taken in their chronological order.

The present Study anticipates to a certain extent, in the matter of the Lectionaries of the Mass, the conclusions which will, it is hoped, be set out and justified in a subsequent Study. The bearing of these Lectionaries on the Kalendar is so important that it could not be omitted or deferred. Meanwhile, until the whole case can be set out, enough evidence is here given to justify various points of detail, and, it is hoped, to create a presumption in the kindly reader's mind that the broad conclusions set out here can also be justified when their turn comes.

WALTERUS TRURON:

TRURO, *Dec.* 1929.

CONTENTS

THE EARLY ROMAN KALENDAR
PART I

PART II

STUDIES IN EARLY ROMAN LITURGY

I. THE EARLY ROMAN KALENDAR

PART I

THE Kalendar in this sense means the list of Saints-days and the like, which are planned to have some liturgical observance, arranged according to the course of the year. Closely connected with it are some other lists made for a different purpose, but useful by way of comparison. Nearest in form lies the Martyrology—a similar list drawn up according to the year's course, primarily in order that a record may be kept of all the martyrs who should be remembered, and of the days on which they are to be commemorated. This aims at being a comprehensive list, not a select list like the Kalendar: but the two kinds of list are often not distinguished; indeed they hardly could be in the early days before Service-books took formal shape.

Another list, useful for comparison in connexion with the Roman Kalendar, is that of the *tituli*—the ancient institutional or parochial churches of Rome; for there was much more likelihood that a martyr would attain to liturgical observance, and so to a place in the Kalendar, if and when there was a prominent church dedicated to the saint. A third list, similar but not identical, is that of the 'Stational' churches in Rome—those where the papal Mass was said with special solemnity on great days. To these may be added a fourth list, containing the names of a few further ancient Roman churches, in which there was indeed no 'station', but in which the clergy collected on certain occasions in order to proceed thence to the stational service. Of less importance, but still worth some notice in this connexion, is the list of the *diaconiae* or deaconries in Rome, the centres of the parochial and eleemosynary administration, superintended by the seven deacons of the city.

Behind all such lists, as the chief source of information lies the *Liber Pontificalis* containing the lives of the Popes. The earliest text that is extant dates from the middle of the 6th century; but this is a Second Edition. The earlier edition, written probably in the time of Hormisdas (514–23), is known through the preservation of two Abridgements.[a] Continuous additions have been made to the original nucleus.

Some study of these data will give preliminary help towards the elucidation of the growth and development of the early Roman Kalendar.

i. *The Martyrology*

The earliest interest in the Martyrology is local, rather than general. Rome is interested in the burial-places of those martyrs that were situated in its numerous cemeteries. The 3rd century saw the beginning of the cult of the martyrs and especially of martyred popes. Popular enthusiasm brought people to their *martyriae*, or sepulchral chapels, on the anniversaries of their deaths for a memorial service.[b] Early in the 4th century an official document was issued which is the ultimate basis of every subsequent Roman development of the kind. That is the so-called Philocalian Kalendar.

It embodies two lists, both dating apparently from 336, but reissued with additions about 354: one contains the *Depositiones Episcoporum*, the memorial days of the popes from Lucius (d. 254) to Julius (d. 352); the other, the *Depositiones Martyrum*. Other revisions have been attributed to the time of Innocent I (401–17) and Boniface I

---

[a] The masterly edition of Duchesne is the one here utilized (Paris, 1886, 2 vols. 4to).   [b] Delehaye, *Culte des Martyrs*, pp. 301 ff.

(418–22).[a] The earliest martyrs recorded there (apart from the Apostles) are those of the 3rd century, beginning with Pope Callistus (d. 222). Earlier statistics are wanting.

At a subsequent date both these lists, enlarged in the course of years, were used to compile the original form of the Roman, or Hieronymian, Martyrology, which belongs to the beginning of the 5th century.[b] The century following produced further additions; and in the 6th century a certain copy of the Roman document, on which all existing texts of the *Martyrologium Hieronymianum* depend, made its way into Gaul, there to receive in the course of the 7th century yet more entries, forming a third stratum. Many of these new entries belonged to the locality, but others were concerned with Roman Saints, and derived apparently from some Roman Service-books, which, like the Martyrology, had made their way into Gaul.

So the Martyrology and the Kalendar met, but apparently in Gaul, not in Rome.

Several attempts have been made to work back from the intricate and conflated text of the Martyrology, as we have it, even in its earliest extant MSS., to the original Roman Martyrology. The work of Kirsch gives the best results in the most systematic form.[c] The list drawn up by him to exhibit briefly the contents of the basic form of the Roman Martyrology, and his list which follows containing the Roman Commemorations added to the earlier form in Gaul, will be continually utilized in this inquiry.

We have thus before us, either as a first source, from which the makers of a Kalendar for liturgical observance

[a] See Duchesne, *Liber Pontificalis* (Paris 1886), vol. i, pp. vi ff. Delehaye, p. 299.

[b] Quentin, *Per la critica del Martirologio Gerolimiano* in *Miscellanea G. B. de Rossi* (Rome, 1924), ii. 103; see *Memorie della Pontificia Accademia*.

[c] J. P. Kirsch, *Der Stadtrömische christliche Festkalender im Altertum* (Münster in W., 1924).

would be bound to draw, or at least as a parallel document, a conspectus of the shrines, distributed about in
the cemeteries surrounding Rome,[a] in which the Roman
Church treasured the memory and anniversaries of its
chief martyrs. Many of these lay near enough to the city
to be easily reached by a solemn official visit on the
appropriate day. Some lay close enough one to another
to be combined in one visit. Together with these suburban shrines there come into consideration a few martyrs
whose shrines are best reckoned as lying within the city,
e.g. St. Peter, SS. John and Paul, in June, and in November the Four Crowned Martyrs, and St. Cecilia.

The greater part of the suburban entries refers to the
great cemeteries situated within 3 or 4 miles of the city;
but a score or so of individual shrines figure in the early
form of the Roman Martyrology which are situated at
a distance of from 6 to 18 miles away.[b] It would be
for the Kalendar to regulate which of these shrines,
numbering about a hundred in all, should be chosen to
receive annually a solemn liturgical visit from the
Roman Court.

ii. *The Tituli*

The *tituli* were the old churches in Rome which were
jointly and severally responsible for the pastoral care of
the city; roughly speaking they may be called parish
churches. They were usually reckoned as 25 in number,[c]
or according to some calculations as 22. There are no

---

[a] The pride of Rome in its urban and suburban shrines is well expressed in
the Leonine Sacramentary, § xiv. 5 a preface of the feast of SS. John and Paul,
'ut non solum passionibus martyrum gloriosis urbis istius ambitum coronares, sed
etiam in ipsis visceribus civitatis SS. Johannis et Pauli victricia membra recon-
deres', &c.   [b] See details below, pp. 24 ff.

[c] The compiler of the *Liber Pontificalis* ascribed this settlement to Marcellus
in 308, 309 (i. 164), but the earlier notices of Cletus (i. 122), of Evaristus
(i. 126), and that of Urban (223–30) a century earlier (i. 143) imply the same.
These entries may be anachronistic. The entry about Marcellus represents
what was, or was supposed to be, the Constantinian plan. This is implied again
in later documents from Hilary (461–8) onward (i. 244).

early official lists, but there are two good lines of evidence. First the signatures of Roman priests to the Acts of the Synods of 499 and 595. Second the lists given in the *Liber Pontificalis* of gifts distributed to each of the *tituli*. This evidence is also supplemented by occasional mentions of the churches, or by monuments of their clergy.

The identification of the names attached to the *tituli* is not always easy. In many of the older Roman foundations the name belongs to the foundation rather than to the church attached to the foundation; and the name is that of the founder. The list of the Synod of 499 is mainly a list of founders' names; but a century later it is clear that there has been a movement for calling the *titulus* after some saint to whom the church of the foundation has been dedicated. The equation of the new name to the old is not always certain, but the following list of 25 *tituli* is approximately correct.[a]

TITLE.	DEDICATION.
Aemilianae	Quatuor Coronati
Anastasiae	Anastasia
Byzantis *or* Pammachii	Johannes et Paulus
Clementis	Clemens
Crescentianae	Sixtus
Equitii	Silvester et Martinus
Eudoxiae	Apostoli *or* Petrus ad Vincula
Praxedis	Praxedis
Nicomedis *or* Matthaei [b]	Marcellinus et Petrus

[a] See Kirsch, *Die römischen Titelkirchen im Altertum* (Paderborn, 1918), or his more popular sketch, *Die Stationskirchen des Missale R.* (Freiburg, 1926): and further study in *Rendiconti Accad. Rom. Arch.* iii. 123 ff. Also Lanzoni, *I titoli presbiterali* in *Rivista Archeol. Christ.* (Rome, 1925), pp. 195 ff.; Huelsen, *Le Chiese di Roma* (Florence, 1927). The titles mentioned in the earlier synod are twenty-nine in number. In one case certainly two names appear for the same church—*Pammachii* and *Byzantis*. This is probably the case also with *Lucinae* and *Laurentii*. Two others, *Matthaei* and *Nicomedis*, probably coalesced in SS. Peter and Marcellinus. *Romani* is otherwise unknown, and is probably also a duplicate. In the later synod only twenty-four names occur, probably because there was no representative of St. Anastasia present.   [b] In 499 only.

TITLE.	DEDICATION.
Eusebii	Eusebius
Pudentis *or* Pastoris	Pudentiana
Vestinae	Vitalis *or* Protasius et Gervasius
Gaii—ad duas domos	Susanna
Cyriaci	Cyriacus
Marcelli	Marcellus
Lucinae	Laurentius in lucina
Damasi	Laurentius in damaso
Marci	Marcus
Fasciolae	Nereus et Achilles
Tigridae	Balbina
Sabinae	Sabina
Priscae	Prisca
Julii et Callisti	Maria trans Tiberim
Chrysogoni	Chrysogonus
Caeciliae	Caecilia

It will be observed that in several cases the founder and the saint are of the same name, but in some of these cases the identity is more apparent than real. It is probably real in the case of Eusebius, for the saint is mentioned in an early form of the Martyrology as the 'founder of the title'. It is otherwise with Pudentiana, for the saint is created out of the title. The term (which is as old as 384) is the adjectival equivalent of *titulus Pudentis*, Pudens being the founder. In other cases when a saint was adopted as patron of a church, one was chosen either because of some local connexion, or through similarity of the name to that of the founder. This was probably the case of the *titulus Chrysogoni*, in which it was necessary to go as far afield as Aquileia in order to find a homonymous saint to be patron: more usually a local saint was brought in.

The saints' names survived, and the founders' names, if retained, were bits of archaism, except when they served to differentiate the churches of St. Lawrence. The cult of the saint acquired a local habitation in the *titulus*, and in most cases[a] this secured also a place for the saint in the Kalendar.[b]

iii. *The Deaconries*

Something must next be said about the *diaconiae*, or deaconries, which from the 7th century onward became important features of Roman church life. The institution was rather that of a parish house than of a parish church. It was the centre of the eleemosynary work of the church in a given district.[c] Most of these establishments were set up in ancient pagan buildings given over to the charitable work; and a number of them accordingly lay in the central districts of the city, unlike the 'title' churches which lay away from the centre.

Their origin is obscure. A first sign is seen in the foundation by Belisarius of the *xenodochium*[d] of St. Mary *in via lata* (*c.* 540). Then *diaconiae* are mentioned as profiting by the Pope's largess[e] under Benedict II (684–5) and his successors, and especially in connexion

[a] Not Susanna or Balbina, except fitfully. Not Sabina at the earliest date.

[b] The estimate of only twenty-two *tituli* was transient, and belongs to the end of the 8th and beginning of the 9th centuries. It is evidenced by the gifts of Popes Hadrian and Leo (*L. P.* i. ccxxxv, 504, 519; ii. 18): and explained by the fact that two *tituli* are under Leo reckoned as deaconries, and a third is unmentioned. One of the two, SS. Silvester and Martin, soon again became a *titulus*; and Sergius II (844–7) had been priest of it (*L. P.* ii. 86, 92). The restoration of the other (SS. Nereus and Achilles) probably followed on the rebuilding of the church by Leo III (795–816); *L. P.* ii. 30. The church of SS. Marcellinus and Peter had been rebuilt by Gregory III (731–41), see *L. P.* i. 420; its omission here perhaps is the consequence of its ruinous condition before the rebuilding.

The history in the 10th century is obscure, and the rise in number to twenty-eight churches—the figure found in John the Deacon, *De eccl. Lateranensi* (*P. L.* CXCIV. 1558). They are arranged in four groups of seven each (Kehr, *Italia Pontificia*, i. 3: and cp. Huelsen, 126). The list includes a *titulus Apostolorum* as well as one *S. Petri ad Vincula*: and adds further St. Cross, and St. Stephen on the Caelian Hill.

[c] *L. P.* i. 364, note 7. *D. A. C. L.*, 'Diaconies'.

[d] *L. P.* i. 296, 300.   [e] *L. P.* i. 364.

with the monasteries. Seventy years later Stephen III
(752–7) interested himself in the old *xenodochia*.[a] He
refounded four (but their names are not recorded); and
he founded three new ones, viz. St. Eustace *in platana*,
and two others situated close to St. Peter's, which he
attached to the ancient deaconries already placed there,
viz. St. Mary, afterwards distinguished as *in caput portici*,
and St. Silvester. The years following seem to have
witnessed more development. Hadrian (772–95) found
16 deaconries existing, and gave gifts to each.[b] He then
founded 2 more (St. Hadrian and SS. Cosmas and
Damian); thus raising the number to 18, which is the
number known to John the Deacon in the 12th century,[c]
continuing down to the 16th century, and still preserved
in the titles of the Cardinal-Deacons. But at times there
were more.

The record of the benefactions of his successor,
Leo III, furnishes a detailed list[d] which amounts to 23.
It included two churches, as has been already noted,
which had been previously, and were again subsequently,
reckoned as *tituli*. If these two are omitted the following
is the list. Notes are added showing how far the *Liber
Pontificalis* attests their existence earlier:

Maria Antiqua (Nova), decorated by John VII (705–
7), i. 385, 386.
Maria in Cosmidi (in schola graeca), Hadrian (772–
95), i. 507.
Maria Dominica (in Domnica), Leo III (795–816),
ii. 8.
Maria in Xenodochio[e] *or* Via Lata; of Belisarius, *c.* 540,
i. 296, 300.
Maria in Achiro (in Cyro), restored by Gregory III
(731–41), i. 419, 424.

[a] *L. P.* i. 440, 456.   [b] *L. P.* i. 504, 520, note 70, 522, note 110.
[c] *loc cit.*, p. 13[b].   [d] *L. P.* ii. 9–12, 14, 16, 19, 21.
[e] But see Huelsen, pp. 365, 376, 377.

Maria foris porta b. Petri *or* in caput portici, founded by Stephen III (752–7), i. 441, 456.

Maria in Hadriano (transpontina), refounded by Hadrian, i. 506, 521.

Luciae in VII vias (iuxta septa solis), Leo III (795–816), ii. 11.

Bonifacii (subsequently St. Alexis), Leo III (795–816), ii. 9. Kehr, i. 115.

Georgii,[a] Leo II (681–3), i. 360, 362.

Theodori,[b] founded probably early in the 6th century; mentioned as a deaconry by Leo III, ii. 12, 21, 41.

Sergii et Bacchii, 1. At St. Peter's founded by Gregory III (731–41), i. 430, 424; it has disappeared. 2. By the Forum, rebuilt by Hadrian, i. 512, 522, note 123.

Cosmae et Damiani, built by Felix IV (526–30), i. 279, added to the deaconries by Hadrian, i. 522, note 110.

Hadriani (in tribus fatis), established by Honorius (625–38), i. 324, 327, added to the deaconries by Hadrian, *ibid.*

Archangeli (in foro piscium), rebuilt in 755 or 770, i. 514, note 2.

Eustachii, the *xenodochium* founded by Stephen III (*ut s.*).

Luciae (in Orphea *or* in capite suburrae *or* in silice), founded by Honorius (625–38), i. 324, 326.

Viti (in macello), found under Leo III as a deaconry; but perhaps mentioned as a monastery under Stephen IV (768–72), i. 470.

Agathae (in equo marmoreo, *or* de caballo *or* in suburra): found under Leo III as a deaconry, and monastery.

Silvestri iuxta b. Petrum, founded by Stephen III, and again by Hadrian (*ut s.*).

Martini iuxta b. Petrum, mentioned under Gregory III (732), i. 422, note 137.

[a] See further below, p. 100.　　　　[b] See below, p. 139.

The list of John the Deacon [a] omits six of these, but gives three others instead, viz.:

Nicholas in Carcere.   The church existed in 1088.[b] Urban II died there in 1099, and it was a *diaconia* at the death of Paschal II in 1118. *L. P.* ii. 294, 313.

Quiricus (Cyriac), probably of the 11th century.[c]

Maria in porticu Gallae, then recently restored by Gregory VII in 1073.[d]

These appear instead of Maria in Hadriano, Maria in caput portici, Boniface, Vitus, Silvester, and Martin.

iv. *The Stations*

Coming to the Stational Churches we find ourselves on definitely liturgical ground. Though we do not yet touch a *Sanctorale*, still less a formal Kalendar, we depend upon liturgical authorities. These papal Stations are first mentioned, as established institutions, in the *Liber Pontificalis* in the life of Pope Hilary (461–8). They were the solemn services held at different churches when the Pope celebrated, supported by the twenty-five parish priests and their people.[e] For ascertaining which were the customary churches, the material available is much less satisfactory because it is of later date, and is largely drawn from sources written outside Italy rather than from purely Roman documents. The Service-books available for this purpose fall into four main classes: (*a*) Sacramentaries; (*b*) Lectionaries; (*c*) *Ordines* or directories; (*d*) Choir-books.

Each of these classes has something to contribute to the

---

[a] Repeated in P. Mallius (Mabillon, *Mus. Ital.* ii. 158), and in Cencio (ibid. ii. 191), but keeping Vitus instead of Quiricus. These are all authorities of the end of the 12th century.

[b] Huelsen, 392.   [c] Ibid., 428.   [d] Kehr, i. 111, 150.

[e] For a possible Jewish origin of the liturgical *statio* see Bonsirven in *Recherches de science réligieuse*, i. 258. The Christian development is set out by Mgr. Kirsch in *Rendiconti*, iii. 123–41. The historical commentary on the rationale of these services given in Grisar, *Das Missale im Lichte römischer Stadtgeschichte* (Freiburg, 1925) is full of interest.

study of the Stational Churches. For the earliest evidence
of Service-books, in the absence of any to be gleaned
from the Leonine Sacramentary (which will be considered presently), recourse must be had to the Lectionaries, for they run back farther than the rest. Four are
extant which stand apart from the rest, because they
represent the stage existing before the second quarter of
the 8th century, when Gregory II (715–31) instituted
Stational Masses on the Thursdays in Lent, where
previously there had been none. The Würzburg lists of
Epistles **We** and Gospels **Wg** and the Jonathan list make
no mention of these.[a] The Reims MS. **R** adds them
in an Appendix. This group of lectionaries is therefore the best available authority for the Stations.

All three will be fully considered in their own right
among the lectionaries at a later point in these Studies.

The list of Stational Churches, visited on days other
than Saints-days, that emerges from these sources, belongs in its existing form to the 7th century; for, while
excluding the Thursdays in Lent, it includes the church
of *S. Maria ad martyres*, which began when Boniface IV
in 609 dedicated the old Pantheon under the said title.[b]
The following list is based upon these three lectionaries;
but additions are entered in a parallel column, and for
these the chief authorities are the Sacramentaries, especially **H**(Hadrian) and **P**(Padua).

STATIONS

The Lectionaries.	*Additions.*
	Dec. 24. Vigil of Christmas. St. Mary Major. **P**
Dec. 25. Christmas.	
1. St. Mary Major (ad praesepe).	
2. St. Anastasia.	
3. St. Peter.[c]	

[a] See for **We** the *Rev. Bénéd.*, xxvii (Jan. 1910); and for **Wg**, ibid. xxviii
(July, 1911). Two other Gospel-lists also, **Jon** & **Qr.**, omit the Thursdays.

[b] On the date see Morin, *Rev. Bénéd.*, xxviii. 327 n.

[c] The Vatican Antiphonal notes *Statio in basilica principis apostolorum: sed*

The Lectionaries.	*Additions.*
	Dec. 28. H. Innocents. St. Paul. **H**
Jan. 1. Octava domini. St. Mary ad Martyres.	
Jan. 5. Vigil of the Theophany. St. Peter.	
	Jan. 6. Epiphany. St. Peter. **H**
Dominica post Theophaniam. SS. John and Paul.	
	After Epiphany.
	i. St. Peter ad Vincula ⎫ in other
	ii. St. Anastasia ⎬ Lection-
	iii. SS. John and Paul ⎭ aries.
Dom. ii post Theophaniam. St. Eusebius.	
Jan. 22. St. Vincent. St. Eusebius juxta Merulana.[a]	
	Feb. 2. Purification or *Ypapanti,* St. Mary Major **H.**
Septuagesima. St. Lawrence foris murum.	
Sexagesima. St. Paul.	
Quinquagesima. St. Peter.	
Ash Wednesday. St. Sabina.	
	Thursday. St. George **H.**
Friday. In Pammachi (SS. John and Paul).	
	Saturday. St. Trypho. Grim.[b]
XL 1. St. John Lateran.	
ii. St. Peter ad Vincula.	
iii. St. Anastasia.	
iv. St. Mary Major.	
	v. St. Lawrence ad Formonsum[c] **H.**

propter brevitatem diei celebratur apud *S. Mariam Maiorem,* Tommasi, *Opp.,* vol. iv, pp. 1-169. Grisar, *Missale,* p. 70.

[a] In **Jon** only: but see also MSS. Amc. Rd. Walt. This church possessed part of the body of a St. Vincent (see Tommasi, *Opp.* v. 440). He was later held to be joint-patron. Huelsen, 251. The observance of the Sunday Station there on Theoph[2]. is also rarely mentioned.

[b] This is the Station that has survived in use. There was variety at first when this day became stational. Fulda Sacr. has *ad S. Mariam,* Zf. has *Ad S. Paulum*: a group of lectionaries (TA., Sp., Krems) has *Ad S. Laurentium in regione tertia.* For this vanished St. Lawrence see Huelsen, 283. It is also called *in Merulana* in Pg.

[c] Some MSS. have *foris murum* by mistake. The later name is *in panis perna*

The Lectionaries.	*Additions.*

XL¹. vi. SS. Apostles.
    vii. St. Peter.

                                  XL². St. Mary in domnica.[a]
                                     VA.OR.

XL². ii. St. Clement.
    iii. St. Balbina.
    iv. St. Cecilia.

                                    v. St. Mary in Trastevere (Callisti) **H.**

    vi. St. Vitalis (ad apostolos inter Vestinae).
    vii. SS. Peter & Marcellinus.

XL³. St. Lawrence.
    ii. St. Mark.
    iii. St. Pudentiana.
    iv. St. Sixtus.

                                    v. SS. Cosmas and Damian **H.**

    vi. St. Lawrence (in Lucina).[b]
    vii. St. Susanna.

XL⁴. St. Cross (In Suxurio *or* ad Hierusalem).
    ii. SS. Four Crowned.
    iii. St. Lawrence in Damaso.
    iv. St. Paul.

                                    v. St. Silvester **H.**

    vi. St. Eusebius.
    vii. St. Lawrence foris muros *or* ad corpus.[c]

XL⁵. St. Peter.
    ii. St. Chrysogonus.
    iii. St. Cyriac (in Thermis).
    iv. St. Marcellus.

                                    v. St. Apollinaris **H.**[d]

    vi. St. Stephen (in Celio monte).

                                    vii. St. Peter **H**, for the Almsgiving: but St. John Port-Latin as Station in OR., &c.

(Huelsen, 292). Pj has Ad St. Andream. The Paduan Sacramentary misrecords the Thursday Stations (see there, pp. 20, 22).

   [a] This was originally *vacat*. The earliest evidence of this station is VA.

   [b] Or ad Titan, **P.**G Ph. S (p. 57): see Mohlberg in *Rendiconti*, iv (1926), pp. 261 ff.

   [c] Changed at a later date (11th cent.) to St. Nicholas in Carcere.

   [d] Theod.¹ has *ad S. Mariam.*

The Lectionaries.	*Additions.*

Palm Sunday. St. John Lateran.
  ii. SS. Nereus and Achilles.[a]
  iii. St. Prisca.
  iv. St. Mary Major.
Maundy Thursday. St. John
  Lateran.[b]
Good Friday. St. Cross (In Hieru-
  salem).
Easter Even. St. John Lateran.
Easter Day. St. Mary Major.
  Pasch. ii. St. Peter.
      iii. St. Paul.
      iv. St. Lawrence.
      v. SS. Apostles.
      vi. St. Mary ad martyres.
      vii. St. John Lateran.
Low Sunday. St. John Lateran.[c]

Litania maior. St. Peter.   Litania maior. St. Lawrence in
                                      Lucina.[d]

Pasch [2]. SS. Cosmas and Damian.[e]

                                   Rogations.[f]
                                   Ascension. St. Peter GG Grim.
                                   Vigil Pent. Lateran GG Grim.
Pentecost.   Pentecost. St. Peter **P H.**
  ii. St. Peter ad Vincula.
  iii. St. Anastasia.

---

[a] For a time the Station was changed to St. Praxedis, see **H**, Spires: but it reverted again later; see VA, OR, and the Compiègne Gradual. But St. Praxedis ousted it again, and figures in the earliest printed Roman Missal (1474).

[b] Theod [1] has *ad S. Petrum.*

[c] So in **We, Jon,** but not **Wg, R.** At a later date (Grim, VA, OR) the entry is *ad S. Pancratium*; presumably this meant the monastery attached to the Lateran, not the Cemeterial church on the *Via Aurelia.* Theod [2] has *ad SS. Cosmam et Damianum* here.

[d] This is properly the *Collecta*: the Mass is at St. Peter's, and there are Stations made at St. Valentine's and the Ponte Molle: then *ad Crucem*, in an oratory of Holy Cross, and on returning at St. Peter's *in atrio.* See the account in *Liber Pont.* ii. 4. But VA, OR give the *Collecta* at St. Maria in Turre near the Vatican.

[e] This is from **We,** and is also in many other sources. But in VA we read *Statio est in basilica S. Petri.* Morin notes that St. Gregory's homily on this day was preached at St. Peter's.

[f] These are later importations into the Roman Rite. The Stations held on the three days according to the modern missal are (i) St. Mary Major, (ii) the Lateran, (iii) St. Peter.

The Lectionaries.	*Additions.*
iv. St. Mary	
v. SS. Apostles.	or *Embertide*[a], St. Mary.
vi. SS. John and Paul.	SS. Apostles.
vii. St. Stephen.	St. Peter.

To this regular list must be added some supplementary indications given in the rest of the year.

June 8. SS. Primus and Felicianus; in basilica S. Stephani.[b] T A. Bre.

June 19. SS. Gervasius and Protasius; ad S. Vitalem. LL.

June 30 SS. Peter and Paul; ad S. Paulum.

July. Octave of the Apostles ; ad Vincula **P H.**

Aug. 1. Statio ad S. Petrum ad Vincula quando catenae eius osculantur GG.

Aug. 22. St. Timothy; ad beatum Paulum apostolum LL.

These indications are not, strictly speaking, directions for a Station but topographical guides as to the church in which a service is to be held. Others will be considered later (p. 29).

At the two other Ember seasons, the weekday fasts have the same Stations as in Lent and Whitsuntide, and these are marked in the earliest Gospel-books. **H** marks a Station at St. Peter's on the Sunday preceding them.

After the September Ember season, the following entry is in **Wg** and **R.**

Ebdomada ii die dominica ad SS.
　Cosmam et Damianum ante na-
　tale eorum (Sept. 27).

[a] The end of Whitsun week varies according as it has not, or has, the Ember days (shown above). The older authorities have them not: see **We** and Staerk, (in the *Comes* printed in *MSS. Latins de St. Pétersbourg* (1910), i. 135–51). At a later date when the Ember days had come into Whitsun week, and Thursday lacked a Station, it was (Grim) provided with one at St. Lawrence Without. But VA gives St. Paul's.

[b] Their bodies were translated to this church from their graves fifteen miles out on the *Via Nomentana, ad arcas*, by Theodore (642–9), *L. P.* i. 332.

The Sundays of Advent belong to the column of late additions. The third, being the Sunday before Ember days, acquired its Station earlier than the first two; and the fourth, occurring on the *Vacat* Sunday, only quite late.

> Advent [1]. St. Mary Major V A.[a]
> Advent [2]. Ad Hierusalem (St. Cross) Grim.
> Advent [3]. St. Peter **P H.**
> Advent [4]. St. Eugenia.[b] OR; VA.

On scrutinizing this list of Stational Churches it will be observed that the places chosen fall into three groups:

(*a*) Nearly all the *tituli* are used; only three of the twenty-five are absent from the list in its early form, viz. SS. Silvester and Martin, St. Praxedis, and St. Mary in Trastevere. All three were subsequently brought in: St. Silvester and St. Mary were utilized for two of the Lenten Thursdays, when they become Stational days; while St. Praxedis for a time competed with SS. Nereus and Achilles on Monday in Holy Week, when that church became a *diaconia* instead of a Stational Church,[c] and finally superseded it.

(*b*) The great patriarchal basilicas of Rome, Constantinian in origin, are especially used, being allotted to the great days; St. John at the Lateran; St. Peter at the Vatican; St. Cross, called Jerusalem, at the Sessorian; St. Paul outside the walls; St. Mary Major, the Liberian

---

[a] Grim has *ad S. Andream ad praesepe*, and so has the Compiègne Gradual (*P. L.* LXXVIII. 641). Another Gradual, Pam, is witness to the second and third. The first three Advent Stations are noted in Ordo Rom. XI (*c.* 1140), *ibid.* 1027. The fourth is added in VA and OR. XVI.

[b] The reference is probably to a cemeterial church in the cemetery of Apronianus on the *Via Latina*, corresponding to the entry on Christmas Day in the Old Roman Martyrology (Kirsch, 43). It was restored by John VII (705–7) (see *L. P.* i. 385); and see farther on the cult of St. Eugenia in Silva-Tarouca, pp. 184–6. It is not clear when the present entry, *ad apostolos*, was adopted. It is given in the printed Roman Missal of 1474 (*H. B. S.*).

[c] Above, p. 13[b], 20[a].

basilica called *ad praesepe*; St. Lawrence, distinguished from the lesser churches of that dedication as *foris muros*, or *ad corpus*; the Apostles, the basilica of that name,[a] not to be confused with the *titulus* Apostolorum, i. e. the Church of St. Peter *ad Vincula*.

(*c*) Some newer foundations; the Pantheon, dedicated as St. Mary *ad martyres* (609), and St. Stephen on the Caelian Hill, called also *in macello* because it was made out of the *Macellum*, or meat-market, by Simplicius (468–83). To these may be added a third, though less well attested as a Stational Church—also a transformed secular building—SS. Cosmas and Damian, constructed by Felix IV (526–30).[b]

Thus the series in its earlier form may go back almost to the beginning of the 7th century.

The later Stations may be divided into two groups: many go back to the 8th century, and are found in the Gospel-books of that date and in the earliest available forms of Gregorian Sacramentary; they are marked with **H** as being in the *Hadrianum* or failing that with **P** (Padua MS.),[c] or with LL denoting groups of Lectionaries. Others of the later column are less well attested, or are less early; and special references are given for them, as also for the variants given in the notes.[d]

The most recent of the churches used for a Station is that of St. Trypho, which first appears in history when rebuilt in 1006.[e]

This list of Stational Churches has an obvious bearing

---

[a] Generally taken to be SS. Philip and James: but called SS. James and John in the *Capitulare Eccl. Ordinis*. See Gerbert, *Monumenta*, ii. 168; and Silva-Tarouca, *Giovanni Archicantor* in *Memorie*, I. ii. p. 194.

[b] *L. P.* i. 106, 279.   [c] See below for **H** and **P**, pp. 52, 57.

[d] The authorities quoted are Grim, the Sacramentary published by Pamelius. F, the Fulda Sacramentary; GG, the Mixed Sacramentaries; Theod ([1, 2]), the Sacramentaries of St. Thierry (for these, see below, pp. 52, 82); VA, the Vatican Antiphonal in Tommasi, *Opp.* iv. 1–169; OR, the late list in Mabillon's sixteenth *Ordo Romanus*, *P. L.* LXXVIII. 1367. Some individual Lectionaries, see the index of authorities.   [e] Huelsen, p. 494.

on the development of the Kalendar. It was natural that the patron saints to whom these great churches were dedicated should have commemorations assigned to them, each on their several days in the church year; though in fact there are some of them which did not secure permanently such a position.[a]

Another group of churches comes gradually into prominence as the places where the *collecta*, or assembly of the people preparatory to a special procession before a Stational Mass, was held. This observance began in a small way with three,—a *collecta* (i) on Ash Wednesday at St. Anastasia; (ii) at St. Lawrence in Lucina on the *Litania maior*; and (iii) on St. Caesarius' Day [b] (Nov. 1) at SS. Cosmas and Damian. At the end of the 7th century there were four processions appointed by Sergius I (687–701) to be held on the newly introduced feasts of the B. V. Mary—Candlemas, Annunciation, Assumption, and Nativity [c]; and then the *collecta* was at St. Hadrian's. These seven *collectae* are found in **H** and also in the Mixed Sacramentaries. When direct Roman evidence becomes again available at the end of the 11th century, these *collectae* and processions have increased in number; three a week are held in Lent. Later on there is added a procession on almost every Lenten week-day, besides other days. *Collectae* accordingly were held at a number of different churches, mainly deaconries. But this evidence is too late to be of service here.[d]

v. *The Suburban Cemeteries and Shrines*

The list of Stations indicates where a great part of the services of the Roman Kalendar take place, viz. those

[a] For example St. Balbina is rarely found in a Roman Kalendar, and St. Susanna only fitfully.

[b] See below, at November 1 (p. 136).   [c] *L. P.* i. 376 ff.

[d] For the earlier condition see Ordo XI, §§ 10–12, 29, 33–5, 72, 74. For the later see Ordo XVI, and the Gradual in Tommasi, *Opp.*, vol. v.

that are held in solemn stational form by the Roman Court. What is the place in the case of other services?

The answer to this question is probably this. These other services are to a large extent prescribed because there is a place in which it is desirable to have a service on a certain day. To a small extent, no doubt, there are some Saints-days included in the Roman Kalendar primarily because it is universally thought desirable to keep such outstanding days; and the question of place is secondary. But in the early times there was little of this point of view. Such outstanding commemorations are chiefly biblical in origin. The Scriptures demanded that there must be a day set apart, e. g. for St. Stephen or for St. John the Baptist being scriptural martyrs. But it is remarkable that the Old Roman Kalendar had at first no feast of the Blessed Virgin, nor any commemoration of the greater number of the Apostles. It was natural as a rule in these outstanding cases to have a church provided for the saint as well as a feast,—though Holy Innocents is an instance to the contrary, and so is St. Timothy, for neither day had a church in Rome linked with it, and the service was held in St. Paul's.[a] St. Cyprian is one of the few non-biblical saints who were commemorated in the Kalendar, though unprovided with a church in Rome. He was very happily united with his rival, the Roman martyred Pope Cornelius, as early as in the Philocalian list. SS. Perpetua and Felicitas were also admitted, as representatives of Africa, into the Philocalian list, but they failed to secure a place in the liturgical Kalendar, and it was probably so for lack of a local habitation in Rome.

Apart from such outstanding cases, an entry is normally made in the Roman Kalendar because there is a place which demands a service on a certain anniversary. The place may be a church within Rome, or a *martyrium* in

[a] Both of them have the direction *ad S. Paulum* in consequence.

a cemetery within reach of Rome. Indeed, we may watch the Kalendar grow, as new churches arise in the city, and claim an anniversary. But the shrines outside belong to the era of persecution, and they do not multiply when that is over. It is worth while then to get an idea of the early places of worship in the cemeteries.

The suburban churches[a] lie at various distances from the city. Some, like St. Paul's and St. Lawrence's, are near enough to be Stational Churches, though they are cemeterial. For the most part the big cemeteries lie within a radius of not more than three or four miles from the middle of the city.

The most famous shrines are in the two cemeteries *Callisti* and *Praetextati* on the *Via Appia*. In the former are venerated St. Callistus himself, with other popes— Fabian, Eusebius, Stephen, Sixtus, and also Cornelius with St. Cyprian; and close by is the shrine of St. Soteris. In the latter cemetery rest SS. Tiburtius Valerian and Maximus, SS. Felicissimus and Agapitus, and St. Urban. Not far off is the cemetery *Ad catacumbas* where St. Sebastian lay, and St. Cyrinus of Siscia. On the *Via Latina* lay St. Gordian. On the *Via Labicana* was the cemetery *Inter duas lauros* where rested SS. Marcellinus and Peter, St. Tiburtius; and St. Gorgonius was farther off. On the *Via Tiburtina*, past St. Lawrence, lay the cemetery called after St. Hippolytus. The *Via Nomentana* starts with the cemetery of St. Nicomede, and then goes on to that of St. Agnes. On the *Via Ardeatina* in *Domitillae* lay SS. Nereus and Achilles; and SS. Marcus and Marcellianus in *Balbinae*. The two branches of the *Via Salaria* lead to St. Hermes, and SS. Protus and Hyacinth, as well as to St. Basilla, in *Basillae*; or else to *Maximi* for St. Felicitas, and to *Thrasonis* for St. Saturninus, and SS. Chrysanthus and Daria. The *Via Flaminia* leads to the cemetery of St. Valentine. On the

---

[a] Cp. Delehaye, *Culte des Martyrs*, pp. 301–33.

Via Aurelia two miles out lay St. Pancras, and near by SS. Processus and Martinian. On the *Via Portuensis* SS. Abdon and Sennen rested in the cemetery of Pontian, Felix a little farther off, and six miles out at the cemetery *Philippi*, SS. Simplicius Faustinus and Beatrice. On the *Via Ostiensis* at *Commodillae* SS. Felix and Adauctus.

On July 10, when the Seven Brothers were commemorated, three services were required—one, *ad Aquilonem*, in the cemetery *Praetextati* on the *Via Appia* for Januarius; the second, *ad Alexandrum*, for Alexander himself with Vitalis and Martial *in Jordanorum*, and for Felix and Philip in the neighbouring cemetery *Priscillae* on the *Via Salaria*; the third, *ad S. Felicitatem*, or in the cemetery *Maximi*, for Silanus.

All these sanctuaries lie in a ring fence close round the city. But some more distant shrines also are brought into the scheme. The observance of SS. Alexander Eventius and Theodulus involved a journey seven miles along the *Via Nomentana* to the cemetery of Alexander; and a journey of eight miles farther was needed for the day of SS. Primus and Felician, in the period before the relics were, for convenience, transferred (in 642) to the church of St. Stephen in the city.[a] It was the first of such translations. A similar case was the above-mentioned one of SS. Simplicius Faustinus and Beatrice, for their relics were translated to St. Bibiana in 683. For St. Basilides a journey of fourteen miles along the *Via Aurelia* was needed; and perhaps for this reason the entry is not very stable in the Kalendar.

St. Cyriac and his companions (Aug. 8) often appear in the Gospel lists without a Gospel; perhaps there had been some unwillingness to go seven miles along the *Via Ostiensis* to their shrine, and thus the status of the festival was uncertain. Other shrines, which were distant, appear fitfully in the lists, such as St. Felicula, seven miles

[a] In the *basilica S. Stephani*, TA Bre.

out on the *Via Ardeatina*; or belong only to the Gelasian tradition, such as SS. Marius and Martha with their children, venerated twelve miles out on the *Via Cornelia*; or SS. Zoticus, Amantius, Irenaeus, and Hyacinth ten miles out on the *Via Labicana*.

It is evident that topographical considerations have been the determining feature of the Kalendar.

The saints of Porto (19 miles) and Ostia (15 miles) are too far off to be taken into account, though they may figure in the early records under the heading *Romae*. Six or seven miles is the limit, and that proves in practice to be too far. So the suburban cemeteries supply names to the Kalendar mainly from the inner ring within a radius of about four miles.

Some names, which might have been so supplied, do not in fact find a place in the Kalendar. Perhaps this was so because the day was already occupied; e. g. on December 25 St. Eugenia cannot compete with Christmas and St. Anastasia takes a subordinate place. But in view of the martyrological record it is surprising that the Kalendar offered no permanent welcome to such martyrs as were venerated at the cemetery *Callisti*,—SS. Parthenius and Calocerus (May 19), St. Pontian (Aug. 13); *ad ursum pileatum* St. Candida (Oct. 3), St. Pimen (Dec. 2); at *Basillae* St. Basilla herself (June 11 and Sept. 22), and St. Maximilian (Aug. 26); at *Castuli* on the *Via Labicana* St. Castulus himself (Mar. 26).

These, and others like them, achieved early fame in the Martyrologies and Cemeteries; but they did not attain the later fame conferred by the hagiologists and the liturgists.

The lists in the Service-books not infrequently insert a topographical note, to make clear the place where the service is to be held. The most noteworthy of these is the note about the Seven Brothers, already quoted. It is found in most of the early Gospel-lists. Others occur sporadically; the **P** Sacramentary is particularly rich in them, as the following list will show:

May 10. Gordian. Via Latina.
　　12. Pancras. Via Aurelia.
　　25. Urban. Via Appia.
June 2. Marcellinus and Peter. Via Labicana.
　　18. Mark and Marcellian. Via Ardeatina.
July 29. Simplicius Faustinus and Beatrice. Via Portuensis.
　　30. Abdon and Sennen. Via Portuensis.
Aug. 2. Stephen. Via Latina.
　　14. Eusebius. Via Appia.
　　22. Timothy. Via Ostiensis.
　　30. Felix and Adauctus. Via Ostiensis.
Sept. 15. Nicomede. Via Nomentana.
　　29. Michael. Via Salaria.
Oct. 14. Callistus. Via Appia.
Nov. 23. Felicitas. Via Salaria.

The occurrence of such notes in the Service-books corroborates the view expressed above, that the shrines in the cemeteries have given rise to the observance of these anniversaries.

At a later stage the outlook changes. The Kalendar is regarded less as a direction where the official Mass will be said, and more as a direction given to a priest serving a church to tell him what Mass he will say there on a certain day. It is not clear by what stages the official Mass at the cemetery was given up. But the main cause is clear enough, viz. the destruction of the Catacombs and cemeteries. And the effect is clear also, viz. that the Curia's directory became the parish priest's Kalendar.

vi. *The Leonine Sacramentary*

The earliest extant Latin Service-book is the so-called 'Leonine Sacramentary', known from a unique MS. of the 7th century preserved at Verona (**L**). It hails from Rome, and dates probably from the middle of the 6th century,[a] and apparently from the Vatican.[b] But this book is in many ways disappointing. It is incompletely preserved. Originally it consisted of 163 leaves; now the first 24 leaves (three quires) are gone. These contained the part belonging to January, February, and March, as well as part of April; so it now begins in the midst of a large group of Masses for Saints-days in April.

The book is divided methodically into sections; there were in all forty-three of these, each containing one mass (group of prayers) or more. The first seven of these sections are wanting, as well as five and a half masses of the eighth section. Calculated either by sections or by pages, the part lost is about one-eighth of the book. But though there is this amount of method, the book is very carelessly put together; even the sections are numbered wrongly, and the masses are often wrongly divided and wrongly numbered.[c]

The book does not attempt to cover the ground of the whole year. There is no provision for ordinary Sundays. Neither the Sundays after Pentecost nor the Sundays in Advent figure in the extant part. There is only Whit-Sunday. The lost part is too small to have contained the Sundays after Epiphany, or the Sundays after Easter up to Ascension Day; nor can it have contained the long set of Masses for Lent.

It is rather hazardous to conjecture what the lost five sections contained; but two of them were probably for Easter Even and Easter Day, corresponding with the Sections x and xi, which provide for Whitsun Eve and Whit-Sunday. Another section presumably was for Epiphany. For the remaining two sections the Octave

[a] See Duchesne's arguments as to date, in *Christian Worship*, ch. v, § 4, p. 135: and Lietzmann's in *Petrus und Paulus*, p. 23.

[b] See VI, § xxxiv, p. 308, or p. 15 in Feltoe's edition (Cambridge, 1896).

[c] For example, § xvi is a mere interpolation into the middle of § xv.

of Christmas and St. Agnes are the most likely candidates; or else the Lent Embertide, in view of the fact that the other three Ember seasons are found at Sections XII, XXVII, and XLIII.

In any case, it is to be noticed that the book begins not with Christmas, nor with Advent, but with January.

This collection of services was clearly written for liturgical use, as one may judge from the size of the page and the fine large uncial writing;[a] it is not to be dismissed as a mere private collection of prayers. The user can even now celebrate or officiate on Ascension Day (§ IX), Whitsun Eve (§ X), Whit-Sunday (§ XI), Christmas Day (§ XL), the Ember Days (§§ XII, XXVII), besides a considerable number of Saints-days. Those that are expressly mentioned or implied are as follows:

June 24. Vigil.
    25. XIII. John Baptist.
    26. XIV. John and Paul.
    29. XV, XVI. Peter and Paul.
July 6. Octave.
    10. XVII. Septem Fratres.
Aug. 2 or 3. XIX. Stephen protomartyr.[b]
    6. XX. Sixtus, Felicissimus, and Agapitus.
    9. Vigil.
    10. XXI. Lawrence.
    13. XXII. Hippolytus (and Pontian). [Agapitus.]
    18. Octave of Lawrence.
    30. XXIII. Felix and Adauctus.
Sept. 14. XXIV. Cornelius and Cyprian. [Euphemia.]
    16. XXV. Euphemia.
    30†. XXVI. Michael.
Oct.   XXXIV. Silvester†. Simplicius.

[a] See the facsimiles in Feltoe's edition.
[b] Note that the Masses of St. Stephen the Protomartyr are given, not at December 26 but at August 2. This is the day of Pope Stephen, as recorded in the Philocalian Kalender, and his obit is actually quoted on this day in the Leonine heading, though the masses which follow belong to the Protomartyr.

Nov. 8. xxxv. The Four Crowned Martyrs.
    21. xxxvi. Cecilia.
    23. xxxvii. Clement. Felicitas.
    24. xxxviii. Chrysogonus (and Gregory).
    29. Vigil.
    30. xxxix. Andrew.
Dec. 24. Vigil.
    25. xl. Besides Christmas the names of seven saints are given in the title, taken from the Old Roman Martyrology.
    26. See No. xix.
    27. xli. John Evangelist.
    28. xlii. Holy Innocents.

This list, it will be noted, in its present form provides for Saints-days by name only in the second half of the year. For the Saints-days of the earlier half there is only whatever may have been in the first five sections (probably only St. Agnes), and the very long and strange collection of forty-three or more[a] Masses for saints, forming Section viii, in the midst of which the MS. in its present condition begins.

This section is a sort of *Commune Sanctorum*: it occupies the position which was often occupied by the Paschal *Commune* in subsequent books; and, like other such collections, it embodies provision for one or perhaps two of the Saints-days of April,—Tiburtius, April 22, and possibly George, April 23.[b] But, apart from this, there is nothing paschal about the collection, except at No. 26. Nearly all the Masses have reference to 'Martyrs', some to 'Martyrs and Confessors', a few to 'Confessors' only, or to 'Saints'. Those applicable to a single saint are rare. No. 17 concerns a female martyr; No. 20 retains the name of St. Lawrence. Four seem to have no reference

[a] Some of the subsections contain two groups.
[b] Gregori in the text of No. 33 is possibly a mis-writing for Georgi. See below, p. 100.

to a saint at all, and among them is one (No. 26) which is purely paschal. No. 34 is concerned with St. Peter, and his basilica, and his relics; and it is headed IN DEDICATIONE.[a]

It is clear that this section has been carelessly put together by gathering into one place a number of Masses from various dates and festivals;[b] but at the same time it makes a very ample provision for the martyrs or confessors who are apparently under consideration. Some grouping of the same sort may be noticed elsewhere. Among the twenty-eight Masses in Section xv for SS. Peter and Paul, a dozen or so are suited quite generally for any apostles; one (No. 21) is a 'Common of all Apostles'; one would suit any group of martyrs. Similarly in Section xvii only one of the nine Masses is proper to the Seven Brothers; some would suit any martyrs, some any Saint's-day. There is no similar grouping for virgins; perhaps this was done in the lost portion, at St. Agnes's Day.

It is this list of saints that is our immediate concern; but in order to understand the book better, it is desirable to note what were the other interests of the user. At Section xviii in July there is a long series of forty-five *Orationes et preces diurnae*, interrupted at No. 31 by *Orationes Matutinae* (four in number) *uel ad uesperum* (3). These are like the later 'Votive Masses'; and with most of them there is a marginal note expressing the 'intention' of the Mass—'for the brethren', 'for the wicked', 'for persecutors', 'in convalescence', 'against vices', 'in thanksgiving', and so forth.

In Section xxviii (September) are placed the Ordination Services for Bishop, Deacon, and Priest. The next Section, xxix, *In natale episcoporum*, provides the bishop

---

[a] The Vatican Kalendar in Tommasi's Antiphonal (*Opp.* iv. 1 ff.) has a Dedication of an altar of St. Peter on March 25, and a *Dedicatio basilicarum Apostolorum Petri et Pauli* on November 18: but neither date seems appropriate.
[b] Three of the Masses (Nos. 39–41) are given in § xiv for SS. John and Paul.

with eight (10) Masses to be said primarily on the anniversary of his consecration by him or his friends. These are followed by fifteen Masses, quite general in character, except one, No. 16, which is marked *post infirmitatem.* It is noticeable that two of the first set are paschal; and several of them are not merely episcopal but papal in character. This seems to indicate that the collection was originally made for a pope; and the indication is confirmed by the reference to St. Peter's already mentioned and a reference to the Lateran Baptistery on St. John Baptist's Day, Section XIII, No. 4.

Before returning to its series of Saints-days the book provides also for the following: xxx Consecration of Virgins; xxxi Marriage; xxxii professedly for times of drought, but including other necessities, especially the protection of Rome; xxxiii and xxxiv the Departed. It is in the last section that Silvester (314–35) and Simplicius (468–83) are named, not as saints, but as popes whose anniversary is to be kept, just as the anniversary of Sixtus III (432–40) may be implied by the invocation there of St. Lawrence; [a] for that pope was buried near St. Lawrence.[b]

Thus a large collection of Masses for various subjects intervenes between the Saints-days of September, and the single Saint's-day set down in October. The saints of November are more fully represented. Five alternatives are given for St. Cecilia (Nov. 22), and seven for the next day. The wealth of alternatives here and elsewhere [c] seems to point to an early state of things, when Masses in abundance were being written, and before the time when any selection was made from the material and stereotyped in the form of a typical sacramentary— Gelasian, Gregorian, Ambrosian, or whatever it might be.

This list of saints is remarkable both for what it con-

---

[a] **L** pp. 146, 147.   [b] *L. P.* i. 235. K. 182.
[c] There are fourteen proper to St. Lawrence.

tains and for what it does not contain. There is no feast
of the Assumption, nor presumably any feast of the
Virgin, except in so far as there may have been an Octave
of Christmas which may have been so regarded. Neither
feast of the Holy Cross is there, nor the Dedication of
the Pantheon (609). The emergence of such things at
first sight seems to suggest that the Sacramentary, as a
book, is older than the MS. of it which has survived.
This suggestion corresponds with the evidence of early
date just mentioned; and there are also other indications
which seem to point to the assigning of at least certain
parts of the collection to the middle of the 5th century;
others to the end of the century, containing quotations
from St. Leo (d. 461), and formulated perhaps in the
time of Gelasius (d. 496).

It must also be remembered that this plan of grouping
masses to form a sort of *Commune* made it possible for
the user of the book to observe any Saint's-day that could
be provided for by a mass drawn from one of the groups.
It must not be argued, therefore, that the user's Kalendar
contained no more saints than those specially indicated.
But it is impossible to say what others, if any, were
in use.

vii. *The Gelasian Sacramentary*

Apart from the *Leonianum* (**L**), there is no MS. of an
early Sacramentary which is purely Roman. The Roman
rite was adopted elsewhere; and of the early MSS. available for this investigation there is hardly any that hails
from Italy, let alone Rome itself. This situation is due,
no doubt, to the devastation of Italy in the earlier Middle
Ages; it is not peculiar to Sacramentaries, nor to Service-
books in general. Consequently books of the Roman rite
written in what we now call France or Germany have to
be scrutinized, and to be made to yield up the secret of
the Roman archetypes on which they were modelled.

This is a very delicate work, and owing to the scantiness of the material any conclusions drawn from it are purely provisional.

It is clear, however, that there are two types of rite which exist side by side, one labelled 'Gregorian' and the other 'Gelasian'. The reason for this association of each type with the name of a great pope will be discussed later.[a] For the moment the terms are mere labels, convenient and traditional, but non-significant.

The earliest available MS. belongs to the type called Gelasian; so it will be convenient to take that type first.

The Vatican MS. Regina 316 (called **V**) is Frankish in origin, and hails probably from the great abbey of St. Denys by Paris. It dates in substance to the end of the 7th century, though palaeographical argument seems to imply that the MS. was not actually written till some decades later.[b] The last two quires have long been detached from the rest of the book.

This MS. stands almost alone; but there exists a fragment of the index of another MS. which was evidently a Sacramentary of the same class. This index is found on two pages prefixed to a Gospel-book, belonging to the 10th and 11th centuries, and hailing from St. Thierry near Reims (now MS. Reims 8). It was probably written at Corbie in the first half of the 8th century.[c]

There is also another fragment, written in a northern-English hand, which probably came from a MS. of this class.[d] These fragments show that the Vatican Gelasian Book may be taken as representing a type.

This impression is confirmed by the Sacramentary it-

[a] See p. 53.
[b] See the latest edition by Wilson (Oxford, 1894). The last two quires are not included in this edition. Their contents, which are supplementary, were printed in full in *Journ. Theol. Studies*, vol. xxvii (1926), pp. 357–74, by Dr. Lowe. The index prefixed to the Oxford edition is not from the MS., but is editorial. The MS. contained an index, but only the latter part of it is preserved, i.e. from Book III, §46. See it in Tommasi's edition (*Opp.* vi. 1) or in *D. A. C. L.*, *s.v.* Gelasien, col. 760.   [c] See *Revue Bénéd.*, vol. xxx (1913), pp. 437 ff.
[d] *J. T. S.*, xii (1911), p. 451.

self. It is very methodically arranged, being divided into three books, having each section numbered, and the whole indexed. After the colophon comes the first of the two detached quires, containing an *Exorcismus contra energumenos*; the second quire contains a penitential and the *Breviarius apostolorum*.

The heading of the First Book proclaims the work to be *Liber Sacramentorum Romanae ecclesiae*; while the colophon at the end of the Third Book runs *Explicit Liber Sacramentorum*. The question at once arises in what sense is the Sacramentary 'Roman'. Its contents, for the most part, include nothing that is inextricably distinctive of the city of Rome or of papal services. In this respect it differs markedly from the Gregorian type. While the bulk of it consists of the series of mass-collects needed for the *Temporale* (Book I), the *Sanctorale* (Book 2), and for Supplementary occasions (Book 3), other materials are worked in. Especially it is to be noted that several *Ordines* have been incorporated, more or less fully, including the rubrical directions characteristic of such *Ordines*. There is an *Ordo* of Penitence,[a] two of Ordination,[b] two of Baptism,[c] and so forth.[d] Now these inserted *Ordines* exhibit more or less signs of Roman origin.

In the opening of the *Ordo* of ordination[e] is found material which is specifically connected with Rome and the Pope.

[a] I. xvi, xv, xxxviii, unlike Mabillon's No. X, but with some resemblance to Silva-Tarouca, p. 187.

[b] I. xx–xxiv has little in common with Mabillon's No. VIII, but is like Gerbert, ii. 39 ff. The other is I. xcv, xcvi.

[c] I. xxix–xxxvi, xlii a, xliv. Compare Mabillon's No. VII. The other is at Whitsuntide, lxvi–lxxvi.

[d] An Order for the Holy Oils, I. xl a, unlike Mabillon, pp. 19, 33, or 97. For Good Friday, I. xli, and Easter Even, I. xlii b, also unlike Mabillon, but like Silva-Tarouca. The remark at the end of xlii b, *orationes . . . sicut in Sacramentorum continetur*, shows that the Ordo is an interpolation. In fact the prayers in question are there, following the remark immediately as § xliii. An Order for the Dedication of a church, I. lxxxviii.

[e] I. xx–xxiv.

§ XX. ORDO QUALITER IN ROMANA SEDIS APOSTOLICAE
ECCLESIA PRESBYTERI DIACONI VEL SUBDIACONI
ELIGENDI SUNT.

*Mensis primi quarti septimi et decimi Sabbatorum
die in* XII *lectiones ad S. Petrum, ubi &c.*

Elsewhere no such clear references as these occur. The
local characteristics have mostly been eliminated, though
the word *pontifex* is not always changed to *episcopus*, and
in one place the usual phrase *Apostolice pontifex* has
survived.[a]

The situation is parallelled in the usual collections of
Ordines Romani, where some are still specifically connected with the Pope and the city of Rome, while others,
though Roman in origin and rite, have dropped out
specific references to the city or the Pope.

We can see here, in the inserted *Ordines*, on a small
scale, and imperfectly carried out, the process which has
apparently been applied on a large scale and more com-
pletely to the rest of the Sacramentary. While remaining
fundamentally a book of the Rome rite, it has been de-
romanized, so far as many details concerning the Pope
and the city are concerned. A comparison with the
Leonianum shows this; for the markedly Roman atmo-
sphere which prevails there is not found in at all the same
degree in the Gelasian.

We next inquire where this process has taken place and
in what interest? Was it done for an Italian or a Transalpine public? This the contents of the Sacramentary
must show, especially when compared with the other
type, the Gregorian, which, as we shall see, belongs
definitely to the Pope and the city.

The contents which concern us in this investigation
are those of the *Sanctorale*; and they throw much light
upon the problem. Happily the fragment of Index
above mentioned preserves that part of the Sacramentary

---

[a] In the deacon's address, I. xxxviii.

which is now needed—the list of the days contained in the *Liber secundus de Nataliciis sanctorum*. It is as follows:

Jan.
14. Felix.
16. Marcellus.
20. Sebastian with *Marius Martha Audifax and Habacuk*.
    Fabian.
21. Agnes de passione.
28. Agnes de nativitate.

Feb.
2. Purification.
5. Agatha.
8. *Thomas the Apostle*.
10. *Soteris*.
14. Valentine *Vitalis Felicula*.
16. *Juliana*.

Mar.
7. *Perpetua and Felicitas*.
25. Annunciation of St. Mary.

Apr.
13. *Euphemia*.

May
1. Philip and James.
3. *Juvenal*.
    Invention of Holy Cross.
12. *Nereus Achilles and Pancras*.

June
2. Peter and Marcellinus.

June
13. *Cyrinus Nabor and Nazarius*.
15. *Vitus*.
18. Mark and Marcellian.
23. Vig. John Baptist.
24. John Baptist.
25. *Vig. John and Paul*.
26. John and Paul.
28. Vig. Peter and Paul.
29. Peter *proprie*.
    Paul *proprie*.[a]
    Peter and Paul.

July
6. Oct. Apostles.
28. Simplicius Faustinus and Beatrice.
30. Abdon and Sennen.

Aug.
1. *Machabees*.
6. Sixtus.
7. *Donatus*.
9. Vig. Lawrence.
10. Lawrence.
11. Tiburtius.
13. Hippolytus.
15. Assumption of St. Mary.
17. Oct. Lawrence.
18. Agapitus.

[a] There follows, Oratio ... de nat. Apostolorum, Vig. Omnium Apostolorum, Nat. Omnium apostolorum.

Aug.

19. *Magnus.*
27. *Rufus.*
28. Hermes.
29. *Passion of St. John Baptist.*

Sept.

1. *Priscus.*
8. Nativity of St. Mary.
9. *Gorgonius.*
14. Exaltation of H. Cross. Cornelius and Cyprian.
27. Cosmas and Damian.
29. St. Archangel.[a]

Oct.

7. *Marcellus and Apuleius.*

Nov.

8. Four Crowned Martyrs.
21. *Vig. Cecilia.*[b]
23. Clement. Felicitas.
29. *Mark*, Saturninus, *Chrysanthus Maurus, and Daria.* Vig. Andrew.
30. Andrew.

Dec.

8. *Octave Andrew.*

The catalogue agrees identically with the *sanctorale* of **V**, except that here St. Thomas is placed on February 8, and Mark is prefixed to the group of saints at November 29. Also, presumably through carelessness, Marcellus (Jan. 15) is put a day too early; at June 18, 19 the vigil and day of Gervasius and Protasius are omitted, and at November 22 Cecilia.

This list shows, by the use of italics, which of the Gelasian feasts are not to be found in the *Hadrianum*, that is the only purely Roman Sacramentary of the Gregorian type which is available.[c] There is none of these distinctive entries that is at all Frankish or Transalpine in character. They are all Roman and Italian in origin and interest. The only trace of Frankish saints to be found in **V** is in the Canon; there SS. Denys, Rusticus, and Eleutherius, St. Hilary, and St. Martin figure towards the end of the earlier list of saints, followed by St. Augustine, St. Gregory, St. Jerome, and St. Benedict.

[a] Ember collects follow.
[b] The feast is omitted.
[c] See further below, p. 52.

The entries then in the *Sanctorale* that are characteristic of the Gelasian V are these:[a]

Jan. 20. Add SS. Marius, Martha, Audifax, and Habacuk.

They are entered in the Early Roman Martyrology as buried 22 miles out on the *Via Cornelia* (K. 47–9).

Feb. 6. Soteris; entered in E.R.M.; buried on the *Via Appia* (K. 49, 50).

14. Add Vitalis; of Spoleto (Lanzoni, 437);[b] and Felicula of Rome, buried 7 miles out on the *Via Ardeatina* (K. 154).

17. Juliana; of Pozzuoli and Cumae.

Mar. 7. Perpetua and Felicitas; Africans, already found in the Philocalian Kalendar.

Apr. 13. Euphemia of Chalcedon.

This is the Eastern date; the Roman date is September 16.

May 3. Juvenal; buried 7 miles out on the *Via Nomentana* (K. 146).

June 12. Cyrinus, bishop of Siscia in Croatia; brought to Rome and buried *ad catacumbas* on the *Via Appia*; but in E.R.M. the date is June 4 (K. 63).

Nabor and Nazarius, the Milanese martyrs. A church near Rome was dedicated to them at the end of the 4th century, 5 miles out on the *Via Aurelia* (K. 63).

15. Vitus of Lucania; probably the patron of the deaconry in Rome (Lanzoni, 320 ff.).

Aug. 1. The Machabees; relics of them were from early days and venerated at Rome in St. Peter's ad Vincula.

---

[a] Note also that there is a Vigil before SS. John and Paul, before SS. Gervasius and Protasius, and before St. Cecilia.

[b] Lanzoni, *Le Diocesi d'Italia* (1927).

Aug. 7. Donatus of Arezzo (L. 568 ff.).

    19. Magnus, bishop of Anagni (L. 157, 166, 300).

    27. Rufus, bishop of Capua (L. 190 ff.).

Sept. 1. Priscus, martyr of Capua (L. 190 ff.).

    9. Gorgonius, a Roman martyr, already in the Philocalian Kalendar; buried *inter duas lauros* (E.R.M.) 4 miles out on the *Via Labicana* (K. 31).

Oct. 7. Marcellus and Apuleius, martyrs of Capua (L. 194 ff.).

Nov. 29. Chrysanthus, Maurus, and Daria, Roman martyrs; their church was in the cemetery of Thraso, not far out on the *Via Salaria Nova.*[a]

These Gelasian Saints-days show no signs of any Frankish influence; and when the entry on May 3 of the Invention of the Cross is also noted, there is no need to regard this as a Transalpine feature. Both the feasts of Holy Cross more probably came into the West from the Greeks of South Italy.[b]

There is a marked interest in suburban Rome itself, different from that shown in the pure Gregorian *Hadrianum*. But another centre of interest is the neighbourhood of Capua. Indeed, the list of peculiar saints which is given above points very definitely to central and southern Italy.

But it must be recognized that, even if the *Sanctorale* shows no sign of Transalpine influence, in the *Temporale* it is otherwise. Not only are notable Roman features absent—such as the Lenten Stations, the *vacat* on the Sundays following ordinations, the Pope's almsgiving on

---

[a] For the epitaphs of Damasus there see Ihm's edition (Leipzig, 1895), Nos. 43, 44, 46, 87.

[b] See them in the Marble Kalendar of Naples in Mai, *Nova Coll.*, v. 58–65. The entries of St. Thomas on February 8 and St. Mark on November 29 are peculiar. Both festivals had various dates at their first introduction. St. Thomas stands at July 8 (?) in Vb and at July 3 in Qk. St. Mark at May 17 in the Neapolitan Kalendar and at April 15. The former date is also given in the Kalendar of Bologna. Kellner, *Heortologia*, iii, § 47.

XL⁵vii, and the *Litania Maior* on St. Mark's Day—but some Gallican features and phrases have been incorporated. For example, while the *Ordo* at I, §§ xx–xxiv is Roman, the other Ordinations described in I, xcv–vi follow a Gallican *Ordo*. Again the terms *Post clausum Paschae* and *Contestatio* (at the end of Book III) are Gallican.

On the whole, however, the amount of Frankish alteration or interpolation in **V** is probably quite small. It seems to be fundamentally Italian; a provincial rather than an urban book; of Roman rite but de-romanized.

The prototype of this Gelasian **V** must have come from Italy to France at the end of the 7th or the early part of the 8th century, if it was an up-to-date book; for any book that claimed to be Roman and up-to-date would after *c.* 740 contain the Masses for the Thursdays in Lent, which are not included here.

The de-romanizing process may have taken place in France when the Gallican modifications were made, or in Italy before the book went out. The former hypothesis seems the less likely of the two, for when next France borrowed a book from Rome it took no steps to de-romanize it. In fact, in any case of the kind, the Roman flavour would be considered an asset worthy of retention, unless, indeed, the early part of the 8th century was very different in sentiment from what we know of the later part.

Of the history of the earlier diffusion of the Roman rite in France very little is clearly known. The process was a very natural one. The wish to do as Rome does is shown as early at 538 in the inquiries made by Profuturus of Braga and the reply of Pope Vigilius.[a] The result was seen in the adoption of the Roman directions[b] at the Council of Braga in 561. This action was abortive, for

[a] *P. L.* LXIX. 15–20.
[b] Bruns, *Canones*, ii. 33, 34. Duchesne, *Christian Worship*, pp. 97, 98.

within a few years the native Spanish rite again recovered its place; but what Braga did unsuccessfully, others were bound to do, and more lastingly, as time went on.

In France no similar de-romanizing action is known to have taken place at so early a date. It is noteworthy that the Old Roman Martyrology came to France at the end of the same century and was adapted to local usage.[a] But this was by way of addition, not subtraction; and indeed this way continued to be characteristic of the welcome which France gave to Italian imports. Presumably the Roman Sacramentary and other liturgical books made the same journey; but the only evidence that we have of this process, as going on in the 7th century, is that of the MS. **V** and the two fragments, which are now under consideration. External evidence of the recourse to Rome for liturgical models does not begin till the middle of the 8th century, and will be discussed later.

In England the position is very different, and the diffusion of the Roman rite is more easily traceable there through the writings of Bede. The mission of Augustine must have brought with it Roman books, but the Celtic christianity, prevailing in the west and in the north of the island, had other traditions, so that at the outset the Roman rite penetrated little way. It was confined to Kent and a small area in Yorkshire, where the Roman missionary, John the Deacon, held his ground. Here, as elsewhere, it was the Roman music which chiefly made way. The rival rite had nothing to compare with it. The Roman music was welcomed and could be adopted for use in conjunction with the traditional rites of the Celtic Church.[b] But its ultimate effect was, naturally, the adoption of other Italian books besides the musical ones.

[a] All existing copies of this rest upon a Frankish revision embodied in an Archetype written at Auxerre or Luxeuil, *c.* 600. Kirsch, p. 4, note 10.

[b] The Irish fragment printed by Bannister in *J.T.S.* ix. 474 has musical items partly belonging to the Roman Chant, and partly not.

A new stage of the diffusion of the Roman rite began in the last quarter of the 7th century. Archbishop Theodore came from Rome, bringing with him Abbot Hadrian of the Niridian monastery near Naples (665). Simultaneously Wilfrid was busy as an active agent for Rome in the north. The days of the Celtic tradition were over, and Roman ways prevailed. Wilfrid brought a teacher of the Roman chant and rite from Canterbury to Northumbria. Meanwhile, Benedict Biscop, the founder of Wearmouth and Jarrow, the joint home of Bede, was making his five journeys to Rome. Then no less a person than John the Arch-chanter of St. Peter's was sent by Pope Agatho to foster this liturgical and musical development, and supervise the revival of the mission generally;[a] and his written directions carried on his work when he himself returned home.[b]

A general adoption of the Roman rite in some form was the consequence of this, and native teachers were trained to carry on the work of the Italians.

A new stage in the acceptance of the Roman rite is shown in the Council of Cloveshoe of 747. The 13th Canon ordered that the services should be conducted *juxta exemplum videlicet quod scriptum de Romana habemus ecclesia.*

England has thereupon a little light to throw on the early diffusion of the Gelasian form of Roman rite. The *Old English Martyrology*[c] of the 8th century notes thus. 'To (June 1) there belong two masses: the former is in the old *sacramentorium,* that is in the Old Mass-book, to the memory of Priscus the martyr: the second is in the New book to the memory of St. Nicomedes the martyr.'

---

[a] See Bede, *Hist. Eccl.,* esp. ii. 16, 20; iv. 1, 2, 18; *Hist. Abb.* 3.

[b] Silva-Tarouca sees the Directory of John in the group of early Roman directions, published by Gerbert (*Monumenta,* ii. 168–71, 181, 183–5 and 177–9), and re-edited by himself. This identification is not justifiable, but the documents are important and the commentary is valuable. See below, p. 50.

[c] Early English Text Society (1911), vol. 116, ed. G. Herzfeld.

Further, it ascribes to the New Mass-book Agapitus (Aug. 18) and Sabina (Aug. 29). To the Old book are further ascribed the following:

Nicander (June 17).	Quintus (Sept. 5).
Magnus (Aug. 19).	Sinotus (Sept. 7).
Rufus (Aug. 27).	Lupulus (Oct. 15).
Priscus (Sept. 1).	Eight names in all.

None of these is in the *Hadrianum*, but the three that are printed in italics are also italicized in the Gelasian list above (p. 40) as being characteristically Gelasian festivals.

Of the eighteen others that form that list seven are also included in the O.E. Martyrology, though they are not there distinguished as belonging to the Old Mass-book; and there may have been three more included, for there is a gap in the Martyrology from January 24 to March 1. These seven are as follows:

January 20, Marius, &c.; March 7, Perpetua and Felicitas [May 3, Invention of the Cross]; June 15, Vitus; August 1, Machabees; August 7, Donatus; August 29, Chrysanthus.[a]

It is observable, moreover, that the compiler only quotes the Old or the New Mass-book as his authority when he has no other information to give. It may therefore be conjectured that some at least of these seven, although he has some martyrological information to give about them and therefore does not need to fall back on the Mass-book for his justification, were also in fact to be found in his copy of the Old Mass-book.

We may, perhaps, press this comparison a little farther. We note that the compiler has no information to give about Sisinnius and his companions (May 29); it is possible, therefore, that he took this entry also from the

[a] The Martyrology also includes on January 23 St. Emerentiana, which will be shown later to be a Gelasian festival (p. 64).

Old Mass-book, though he does not say so. The same is true of Aristion of Capua[a] (Sept. 3); and the guess in this case is more secure, for it was from Capua that came all the last five saints out of the seven ascribed to the Old Mass-book.

Becoming thus interested in the geographical affiliations of all these seventeen entries in the O.E. Martyrology, we note that while six are Capuan, Nicander is a martyr venerated at Venafro, Naples, and Capua; Magnus points to Anagni; Donatus to Arezzo.[b]

This sets us inquiring what else there is in the O.E. Martyrology that suggests affinities with Central and Southern Italy.

For Central Italy we observe:

June 29. Cassius of Narni (d. 558) (Lanzoni, 404).
July 10. Anatolia of Tora in Picenum, in the Sabine territory (L. 347).

For Southern Italy—besides the group of Capuans:

Apr. 18. Eleutherius of Troja (Aeca) in Apulia (L. 268).
Aug. 12. Euplius of Catania in Sicily (L. 624 ff.).
Sept. 15. Mamilianus of Palermo (L. 645–9; cp. 523–5).
    19. Januarius of Naples, and
    23. Sosius of Misenum, his companion (L. 214).

These are not names of more than local importance; their occurrence, therefore, in an English Martyrology is significant. The exact relation of this Martyrology to this Kalendar is not fully clear, but they are evidently closely connected. Moreover, each of them must have had the same sort of Italian provincial flavour as the known Gelasian **V**.

A confirmation of this evidence is found in the Kalendar of St. Willibrord,[c] written in the first quarter of the 8th century. Of the names in the Gelasian list

[a] Lanzoni, 190.
[b] See Lanzoni, 166, 176, 387. The Priscus of June 1 is not so far identifiable.
[c] Ed. Wilson (*H. B. S.*, 1918).

(p. 40) there appear Juliana, Invention of H. Cross, and the Machabees in the original hand; and there is an entry of Januarius (above) which is also original. Among those added at a slightly later date were Vitus, Donatus, and Priscus (Sept. 1) of the Gelasian set; and of those ascribed in the Martiloge to the Old Mass-book, Priscus (June 1), Nicander (June 17), Quintus, Sinotus, and Lupulus. Of the last list just given not only Januarius (p. 48) occurs, but also, in the later hand, his companion Sosius. Thus the Gelasian influence reappears, and the influence of provincial Italy also, and of Capua especially. Indeed, there are found here three additional Capuan entries,[a] Agapitus (Jan. 14), Augustine and Felicitas (Nov. 16),[b] Nicander Cassian and Felicissimus (Nov. 26).[c]

A further corroboration is brought by the Lindisfarne Gospel-series. This list of liturgical Gospels, found in that famous MS., and existing also in part elsewhere, includes among the Holy-days for which provision is made three of our characteristic Gelasian entries—The Invention of Holy Cross, the Vigil of SS. John and Paul, and St. Vitus, as well as St. Januarius. Thus it represents an affinity with Campania and Southern Italy.[d]

Additional confirmation is found in the Martyrology of Bede. This, in its authentic form,[e] contains Marius, &c. (Jan. 20), Emerentiana (Jan. 23), Juliana (Feb. 16), Perpetua and Felicitas (Mar. 7), Donatus (Aug. 7), Euplius (Aug. 12), Januarius (Sept. 19), Sosius (Sept. 23) among those on our Gelasian list. This seems to show his use of an Old Gelasian rite; and the Capuans in

---

[a] Lanzoni, 190 ff., 196, 198.   [b] See below, p. 66.

[c] Also in Angoulême Sacramentary.

[d] See Morin in *Rev. Bénéd.*, viii (1891), 481 ff., 529 ff.; x (1893) 113–26. Also *Liber Comicus*, pp. 426–35. Morin cites, as well as Nero D. iv, the Lindisfarne book, another MS. of the British Museum, Royal I. B. viii. A third witness to the same series may be found, though incompletely, in Reims MS. 9.

[e] As restored by Dom Quentin, *Martyrologes Historiques* (Paris, 1908), pp. 17–119.

September point to its having been one like that which
we have noted as prevailing in England.

All combines to prove that the Old English Mass-book
must have been one which came to the north of England
in the enthusiastic days of Theodore and Wilfrid of
Abbot Hadrian and St. Benedict Biscop in the last
quarter of the 7th century, and one which had many
affinities with the known Gelasian.

This date is also what we should suppose, from **V** and
the fragmentary Index, to have been the time when the
Gelasian came to France. There may be more than a
mere coincidence in this.

But what was the New Mass-book? and was it connected with the fresh stage of adoption of the Roman rite
to which the Council of Cloveshoe in 747 bears witness?
All that can be said is that the three festivals mentioned
as characteristic of it, Nicomedes, Agapitus, and Sabina,
will be seen hereafter to figure both in the Gregorian
and in the Mixed Sacramentaries, while the first and
third are absent from **V**.

Returning now to France we note a great lack of
evidence as to the impact of the Roman Liturgy there
in the 7th century, when the influence was so marked
in England. The native Gallican liturgies were clearly
being influenced by the Roman rite. There are few
surviving Gallican books which do not show signs of that
influence. But there is little else to illustrate the conflict.

We note further that another liturgical discipline also
has been imported into France and flourishes there. It
also comes into conflict with the Roman rite there and
elsewhere. This is the Irish tradition prevailing wherever
St. Columban and his followers penetrated. In this
particular conflict it was ranged by kinship on the side
of the native Gallican rite and against the Roman. The
conflict has left behind it but few clear indications of the

struggle and of the ultimate compromise by which the Roman rite won the day.

The chief surviving piece of polemic is the epilogue to the Roman directories re-edited recently by Silva-Tarouca. He, indeed, regards this epilogue as the protest of John the Roman Arch-chanter written in England, *c.* 680, and aimed against the Celtic and Irish traditions prevailing there. But the directories in question can hardly be, in their existing form, of earlier date than the 8th century; so that attribution to John must be rejected as unconvincing. Still, it must be recognized that the author of that epilogue is a man expert in the customs of Rome. He cites indignantly, as the authorities which justify his contention, no less than eight popes, ranging from Damasus (d. 384) to Martin (d. 654), and three subsequent abbots of the Monastery which served St. Peter's at Rome. The enemy against whom this wealth of authority is deployed is surely Gallican. They are people who claim to follow not a Celtic tradition but that of SS. Hilary, Martin, German, Ambrose, and others. The *terra occidentalis*, to which the Epilogue claims that these very saints were sent by Rome, is not England but Gaul. It is France, not England, that is the *pars ista occidentalis seu et aquilon(aris)*, from which the irate romanizer anticipates an obstinate resistance, which will be reckoned as the seventh great heresy foreshadowed by the Apocalypse.

If this is a more tenable explanation than Silva-Tarouca's, what we have here is a fine specimen of the warfare in which the Gallican rite was defeated.

The conflict of Rome with the Columban tradition is illustrated, from the other side, in the Celtic claim to follow apostolic tradition. This claim is elaborated in the account that an Irish monk has left of the liturgical world as he saw it in the 7th century. In it he describes the *Cursus Romanus* and its entry to Gaul; the *Cursus Gallorum*, which derives from St. John the Evangelist;

next, and at great length, the *Cursus Scottorum*, derived from St. Mark; and finally, *Cursus alius Orientalis*, *Cursus S. Ambrosii*, and *Cursus S. Benedicti*.[a] This account, too, is a piece of polemic; and it illustrates the struggle. Little more is known of it; but what clearly emerges is the victory of the Roman rite and a period of fusion represented by the mixed Gallican books.

viii. *The Gregorian Sacramentary*

We turn on again to France. There, if the movement of diffusion of the Roman rite at the end of the 7th century is obscure, it is otherwise with the middle of the 8th century, which in France as in England is an epoch of romanizing in Liturgy, and of a strenuous effort to supersede the mixed Gallican books by the authentic Roman rite.

It was the moment when Pippin, seizing the power, sought sanction for his action from Rome. Chrodegang, appointed by him Bishop of Metz in 742, was his chief agent in this, and his main emissary to Rome. In 752 the Pope Stephen was persuaded to visit France. In these circumstances a fresh interest in the Roman rite was natural. The Roman chant again paved the way for the introduction of the Roman Mass. Metz, under Chrodegang, became the centre of the movement; and the widely spreading influence of Chrodegang and his reforms in clerical and cathedral life diffused an eagerness to conform strictly to Roman services.

Thirty years later Charlemagne gave a fresh impulse to the movement. We do not know what form of Mass-book came in under Pippin; but when Charles, confronted with mixed books of much variety, asked Pope Hadrian to send him a model,[b] he sent him a book which

[a] See Haddan and Stubbs, *Conc.*, i. 138, and cp. Silva-Tarouca. Warren, *Celtic Church*, pp. 77–80.
[b] Hadrian's reply is in *Codex Carol.*, Ep. 92 (*MGH.*, Epp. iii. 626). The date lies between 784 and 791. The earliest extant MS. of the Sacramentary, which

he described as *immixtum*. This is identifiable with that form of Gregorian Sacramentary which is now described as the *Hadrianum*, being a purely Roman book.

A table of the Hadrian Sacramentary. **H**

I. In its pure form it is found in two extant MSS.[a]

C. Cambrai MS. 164. Sacramentary of Bishop Hildoard (written in 811). Leroquais 4. Edited by Wilson (*H. B. S.* 1915), and Lietzmann (Münster 1921).

Non. Paris Bibl. Nat. MS. Latin 2292. Given[b] to Nonantola Abbey, *c.* 876. Leroquais 10.

This Sacramentary was found to be deficient, and Alcuin was brought in (*c.* 800) to supplement it, in order to meet the needs of the Frankish church.

II. **H** is found separate, but followed by the supplement of Alcuin in the following MSS.:

R. Rome. Vat. MS. Regin. 337. Middle of 9th cent., Frankish. Used by Wilson *ut s.*

O. Rome. Vat. MS. Ottob. 313. First half of 9th century; probably from Paris: used by Wilson *ut s.*

Rod. Paris. Bibl. Nat. Latin 12050 from Corbie. 'Sacr. of Rodrad'. *c.* 850. Leroquais 9.

Arel. Paris. Bibl. Nat. Latin 2812 from Arles: late 9th cent. Leroquais 20.

Belv. Paris. Bibl. Nat. Latin 9429 from Beauvais: 10th cent. Leroquais 25.

Marm. Autun MS. 19. From Marmoutier: *c.* 850. Leroquais 14.

Cen. Le Mans MS. 77. Second half of the 9th century. Leroquais 11.

III. Later Gregorian books, formed by the fusion of Hadrian and the Alcuinian Supplement, with or without further additions, are the normal Sacramentaries of the 10th and 11th centuries.

IV. Noteworthy is a combination of Hadrian (slightly altered) with a different supplement in

Theod. Reims MS. 213. 'Sacr. of St. Thierry': second half of the 9th century: Leroquais 8.

V. This supplement is fused with Hadrian in

Grim. Cologne MS. 88. 'Sacr. of Grimold': edited in Pamelius *Liturgicon.*

(we suppose) was sent, is of 811. With it presumably there came also the Antiphonal, of which Amalarius speaks in his prologue to the *De Ordine Antiphonarii Liber*, as being *ordinatum prisco tempore ab Adriano Apostolico.*

[a] Perhaps there should be added to these the palimpsest fragment published by Dold as *Ein Vorhadrianisches Greg. Palimpsest-Sakramentar* (Beuron, 1919).

[b] *Speculum*, i, p. 62.

The foregoing table shows the line of development which this Roman Sacramentary was to take, starting from **H**. The future lay with it, though its victory over the Mixed Sacramentaries was slow, and was only won by adopting, first in a supplement and then into itself, much of the Gelasian and Gallican elements of its rivals. But we are more interested in going backwards to know what the previous history of this type of Roman Service-book had been. Its heading proclaims it to be . . . *Liber Sacramentorum de circulo anni expositum a S. Gregorio Papa Romano editum ex authentico libro bibliothecae cubiculi scriptum . . .*, but we are left doubting how such a heading is to be understood. Nearly two centuries had passed since St. Gregory's death (604); in the interval St. Gregory's own mass has been inserted; and what further? How can we get to the earlier stages of the Gregorian Sacramentary?

Before attempting this, we, taking our stand on the Gregorian tradition, can repeat the question, postponed above, as to the justification of the term 'Gelasian' applied to the other tradition. Hitherto no known book claims the title. It becomes known to us, as the description of a whole Sacramentary[a] or of a liturgical formula, only after the *Hadrianum* has reached France. It certainly is not historically justifiable. In the earliest form which we have, not only it cannot refer to the time of Gelasius (492–6), but it is subsequent also to St. Gregory. It seems as though the term came into use in order to describe Roman books and formulas which differed from type newly received, of which **H** is the standard. The *Liber Pontificalis* in its life of Gelasius had ascribed to him some liturgical activity;[b] and this seemed to justify

[a] The *Sacramentarium Triplex* (Tr.) is our earliest evidence, if it is of the end of the 8th century. Most of the evidence is of the 9th century or later.

[b] Fecit etiam et sacramentorum praefationes et orationes cauto sermone, *L. P.* i. 254.

the ascription to him of the older Roman type.[a] There may have been some better justification than this, but at present we know of none; though Gelasius is one of the eight popes cited by the author of the epilogue mentioned above as one who *omnem annalem cantum . . . conscripsit.*

Hadrian's book **H** was, in any case, not a great credit to the sender. It was a rather careless compilation. Like the *Leonianum* and the old Gelasian **V**, it was divided into numbered sections; but the numbering was very carelessly done. In consequence few of the MSS. show any trace of this numbering, and it is only partially preserved.[b]

The contents are not orderly. After the opening, with the Canon, there follow some prayers of ordination before the main part of the book begins with the Mass of Christmas Eve. The Saints-days are set in five main blocks, following Christmas Day, Epiphany, Low Sunday, Ascension, and the Sunday after Pentecost; but the fifth block is divided by the insertion of the Ember days of September with two Sundays, one preceding and one following them. The Sundays of Advent come after this block, with St. Lucy inserted after the Second Sunday, and the Ember days between the Third and the Fourth. The book then provides for the Dedication of a Church. Two masses follow for a pope to say, one on his *dies natalis*, and the other on the anniversary of his ordination to the priesthood. Then a nuptial mass, a considerable collection of miscellaneous collects, and a collection of the episcopal prayers to be said at Occasional Offices; intercessions in time of war, drought, plague, and other troubles. Then is added a mass for a pope to say on behalf of his predecessors; and lastly, as an after-thought, the alterations are given which must be made, in the

[a] See further on this, Baumstark, pp. 7–21, in his Essay added to Mohlberg's edition of **P** (Münster in W. 1927).
[b] See the reconstruction in *J. T. S.*, vol. xviii (Oct. 1916), pp. 47–55.

prayer (given at the beginning) for the consecration of a bishop, when the person consecrated is to be pope.

Far more serious than the disorderliness was the defectiveness of the volume. It made no attempt to provide for the lesser Sundays of the year—those following Christmas, Epiphany, Easter, and Pentecost;[a] though it provided for Advent. This defect in itself was sufficient to render the Sacramentary inadequate for its purpose in France, and to make some supplement necessary if the book was to be in general use. It is quite possible that the lack of these Sundays in **H** was not due to carelessness; the book being meant only for personal use, and calculated to serve for those special days when the Pope said a Solemn Mass. There are signs after Christmas that its archetype contained the lesser Sundays.[b] But this matter is not relevant to our present subject, which is the Kalendar of the Book.

The Saints-days needed and received no additions from Alcuin, except that a *Commune sanctorum* was included in the Supplement. This was required in order to provide for those Saints-days, which in France it was customary to observe, but for which no provision was made in the Roman *Sanctorale* contained in the Sacramentary. From that *Sanctorale* we can gather the Kalendar, as it was being used in Rome at the time of Charlemagne. And indeed we have already taken some notice of this (p. 40), in estimating, what part of the Gelasian Kalendar was peculiar to that type, and what part it shared in common with the Gregorian type. We are, however, concerned further to ascertain what development of the Gregorian list of saints had previously taken place in the 7th and first half of the 8th centuries, and thereby to ascertain, as far as possible, what the original form of the Gregorian Kalendar was. In other words we desire to

---

[a] Except what it provides for the Ember Sundays in summer and autumn.
[b] *Sacr. Gregorianum* (ed. Wilson) p. 16.

get behind the *Hadrianum* for this purpose. This is a very
difficult task.[a] As we shall see later, the course of that
development is far more easily ascertained from the
Lectionaries than from the Sacramentaries. But before
we pass on to them, the problem as it concerns the
Sacramentaries must be briefly handled. The trouble is,
that not only is there no Italian manuscript of the
Gregorian Sacramentary of earlier date than the *Hadrianum*,[b] but that there is no complete Gregorian MS., from
France or elsewhere, which can be definitely dated
earlier than **H**. There is a fragment, and possibly more
than one, which shows that the supposition that the
Gregorian rite at an earlier stage was fuller and more
adequate than the *Hadrianum* is no fancy; but the MSS.
fail us; and beyond indicating that the sort of book that
we are seeking really did exist, they tell us very little,
so far as they are at present available.

ix. *The Mixed Sacramentaries*

There is, however, another line along which it is
possible to move with a view to deducing what the earlier
stage of the Gregorian Sacramentary was like. There is
in existence a number of Sacramentaries which represent
a blend of the Gelasian and Gregorian. It has been
customary to regard them as Gelasian, and indeed they
were so named in their own day, on the principle that
whatever is not Gregorian pure and simple, is to be
called Gelasian. But for the purposes of our inquiry it is
necessary to emphasize that this considerable group of
Sacramentaries represents a Gregorian book which has
received Gelasian modification, and not a Gelasian book
which has been Gregorianized. It is sufficient merely to
look at the structure of the three types of book to see that

---

[a] Lietzmann's edition is an attempt at reconstruction: see Wilson's criticism
of the effort in *J. T. S.*, xxiii (1922), 392.

[b] There is a fragment from a palimpsest Sacramentary at Monte Cassino. See
Rev. Bénéd., xxvi (1909), pp. 281–300.

this is the case. The Gelasian order, which divides the Sacramentary into three books, with the saints collected in the second, and separated from the *Temporale*, does not rule in this class of Mixed Sacramentaries. The order is that of the Gregorian—namely, a single book with the saints interspersed in groups at different places during the course of the year. All the so-called 'Gelasian' Sacramentaries, other than the one mentioned above (**V**), are of this mixed character.

Mixed Sacramentaries evidently, as we may judge from the surviving volumes and fragments, were spread over a wide area.

The Frankish tradition is seen in the following complete books.

I. **P.** Padua MS. D. 47, printed in abstract by Mohlberg:[a] written perhaps at Liége (841–55), and taken to Verona (961–74).

G. Paris, Bibl. Nat. MS. Latin 12048. Sacramentary of Gellone; described in *D. A. C. L. sub voc.* Gellone and in Leroquais 2.

A. Paris, MS. Latin 816. Angoulême Sacramentary,[b] printed by Dom Cagin. Leroquais 3.

R. Zürich, Kantonalbibl. MS. 30. Rheinau Sacr., but Frankish in origin, given in outline by Wilson:[c] of the 8th century: with a small *Sanctorale* only.

Ph. Berlin, Phillipps MS. 1667, described in *Ephemerides Liturgicae* (1929).

Re. A Reims Sacramentary published by Chevalier[d] from a late transcript of a lost MS., written 797–9.

II. The German Tradition is seen in these:

S. St. Gall MS. 348; St. Gall Sacramentary: given in outline in Wilson, *Gelasian Sacr.*, and printed in full by Mohlberg.[e] Probably written near Chur, *c.* 800.

Tr. Zürich Stadtbibliothek MS. C. 43. The *Sacramentarium Triplex* of Gerbert:[f] written at St. Gall.[g] The Gelasian material is almost the same as in G above, and is taken from a similar MS. It belongs

---

[a] *Die älteste erreichbare Gestalt des Liber Sacramentorum,* &c., published in *Liturgiegeschichtliche Quellen,* No. 11–12 (Münster in W., 1927).

[b] Société Hist. et Archéol. (Angoulême, 1919).

[c] *Gelasian Sacr.,* ut supra.   [d] *Bibl. Liturgique,* vol. vii (Paris, 1900).

[e] *Das Frankische Sacr. Gelas.,* &c., published in *Liturgiegesch. Quellen,* ut supra, 1–2 (1918).

[f] *Monum.,* i. 1–330 (St. Blaise, 1777).   [g] *D. A. C. L.,* vi. 240.

to the early years of the 9th century, or (more probably), is a copy of a MS. of that date.

F. Much later, but still of this type, is the Fulda Sacramentary:[a] printed by Richter and Schönfelder from Göttingen Univ. MS. Theol. 231.

III. There is also an increasing group of Fragments, rescued from bindings, palimpsests, and the like. Dold has published a considerable portion of a Reichenau MS., as well as smaller fragments.[b] These seem to belong to a different type of Mixed Sacramentary, much more restricted in its contents alike in the *Temporale* and in the *Sanctorale*.

The most considerable Fragment is the Palimpsest published by Mohlberg[c] from the Angelica MS. at Rome, no. 1408. It is said to be of Italian provenance and to be allied to the (unpublished) Sacramentary of Monza. Thus the Mixed Sacramentaries must have found their way back to Italy. Indeed it is clear from the additions made to **P** after it came to Verona, that the more developed Gelasianizing was in favour there.

IV. The existence of Mixed Sacramentaries of this sort in England seems to be shown by the fragment contained in Paris, Bibl. Nationale Lat. 9488 published by Bannister.[d]

V. The eastward extension of the Roman rite calls for a word of notice, though the subject is little explored as yet. Various Slavonic versions show some prevalence of the Roman and Gregorian tradition in the Balkans. Two versions in Glagolitic script are known of the Canon of the Mass. See (*a*) Успенскій, i.e. Bishop Porfiry of Chigirin, Второе Путешествіе (1858–61), pp. 180 ff., and (*b*) Кекелидзе, Литургическіе Грузинскіе Памятники (Tiflis, 1908), p. 203. The latter text is very interesting and includes an Invocation of the Holy Spirit in the *Te igitur*. More directly pertinent here is the fragment of a Roman Mass-book published originally by Срезневскій (see Сборникъ of the Petersburg Academy, Section for Russian Language and Literature, vol. xv (1877), p. 529), and again by Jagič in his *Glagolitica* (Vienna Academy, 1890, vol. xxxviii), lastly by Mohlberg in *Memorie, Pontif. Acad. di Arch.*, vol. ii, pp. 207–320; with facsimile of each of the seven leaves.

These leaves at Kiev may have been part of a Sacramentary, as they contain masses of St. Clement and St. Felicitas (Nov. 23), followed by six masses for the year, one of martyrs, and one of the heavenly powers. But the first leaf, preceding St. Clement, contains in a later hand an extract from the Acts of the Apostles and a prayer from Lady-day.[e] The Saints'

---

[a] (Fulda, 1912).

[b] *Palimpsest Sakramentar*, in the *Texte und Arbeiten* of Beuron, vol 12 (1925). See also others in *Jahrb. für Lit.*, iii.

[c] *Atti della P. Accad. Rom. di Archeol: Rendiconti*, iii. pp. 391 ff. (Rome, 1925.)   [d] *J. T. S.* ix (1908), 398–406.

[e] Protege domine famulos tuos (*P. L.* LXXVIII. 52).

masses are mainly Gregorian. The others are very similar to **P**. It is more likely that the leaves represent, not a Sacramentary, but merely a set of extracts. And it may be that the great interest in St. Clement prevailing in the mission of SS. Cyril and Methodius was the cause why the little collection contained the masses of November 23.

The Mixed Sacramentaries in the main follow the Gregorian plan of arrangement, except that they put the Canon at the end. They are, however, as befits amalgams, not very uniform in their contents. Indeed very slender acquaintance with them shows that the extent to which the Gregorian model has been altered in a Gelasian direction varies with each particular MS. For example, one will keep the Gregorian construction of the Mass, that is to say, will have only one Collect instead of the two which are customary in the Gelasian Mass; while another will to a large extent adopt the two Gelasian Collects. This is a broad generalization descriptive of this group of MSS. A further inquiry into detail would reveal that the amount of borrowing from Gelasian sources varies very much,[a] and that these Mixed Sacramentaries had borrowed from other sources besides what we know as Gelasian—possibly from the Ambrosian rite.[b]

Confining ourselves again to our special subject, namely, the List of Saints and the Kalendar, it is naturally the first thing to inquire into the differences between the *Hadrianum* and the least Gelasianized Sacramentary, and then to compare those MSS. in which there has been a larger adoption of Gelasian days into the Gregorian *Sanctorale*. The Mixed Sacramentary now at Padua **P** is the one which is least modified in the Gelasian direction. So it would be well at this point to have before us, as a standard of comparison for the Gregorian rite,

[a] See the important study by Hohlwein, *Untersuchung über die überlieferungsgeschichtliche Stellung des Sacr. Greg.* in *Ephemerides Liturgicae*, xlii (1928), 231 ff. 444 ff.: and compare Andrieu in *Revue des Sciences Religieuses* (Paris, 1922), pp. 197–210.

[b] Baumstark, ut supra, pp. 120 ff. More probably Milan was the borrower.

a list of the Saints-days, as they are found arranged in blocks within the *Hadrianum*, and also, side by side, a list of the Saints-days of **P** set out according to their distribution week by week through that book.[a]

First half-year

H P After Christmas; St. Stephen, St. John Evang., H. Innocents, St. Silvester.

H After Epiphany; Felix, Marcellus, Prisca, Fabian, Sebastian, Agnes, Vincent, Agnes *secundo*; Hypapante, Agatha, Valentine; Gregory, Annunciation.

    P After Epiph[1]., Felix; Epiph[2]. Marcellus–Vincent; Epiph[3]., Agnes 11⁰; Epiph[4]., Hypapante, Agatha; Epiph[5]., Valentine [no Gregory].

    After Low Sunday and Pascha Annotina; the Annunciation.

H After Low Sunday; Tiburtius and Valerian [and Maximus], George, Litania Maior, Vitalis, Philip and James, Alexander Eventius and Theodulus, John Port-Latin, Gordian and Epimachus, Pancras, Mary ad martyres.

    P After Oct. Pasch[1]. Tiburtius Valerian and Maximus.

    After Oct. Pasch[2]. [no George]; Litania maior, Vitalis.

    After Oct. Pasch[3]. Philip and James, Alexander, &c., *Invention of H. Cross.*

    After Oct. Pasch[4]. John Port-Latin, Gordian (without Epimachus), Pancras, Mary ad martyres.

H P After Ascension; Urban.

---

[a] The distribution in **H** is arbitrary and not consistent with any actual year. The two lists that follow are combined in one view, the entries proper to **P** being indented.

Second half-year

H After Oct. Pent. series from Nicomede to Euphemia, Lucy and Geminian (see below).

   P After Oct. Pent. Nicomede, Marcellinus and Peter.

     After Pent[3]. Mark and Marcellian, Protasius and Gervasius.

     After Pent[4]. Vigil John B., Nat. J. Bapt. (2), John and Paul.

     After Pent[5]. Vigil of Peter and Paul, Peter, Paul, Processus and Martinian.

     After Apost[1]. Oct. Apost., Septem Fratres.

     After Oct. Apost[123]. Felix, &c., Abdon and Sennen.

     After Apost[4]. Stephen, Sixtus, Felicissimus and Agapitus.

     After Apost[5]. Cyriac, Vigil, Lawrence (2), Tiburtius, Hippolytus.

     After Lawr[1]. Eusebius, Assumption, Agapitus.

     After Lawr[2]. Timothy.

     After Lawr[3]. Hermes, Sabina, *Passion of John Bapt.*, Felix and Adauctus.

     After Lawr[4]. Nativity of B.V. Mary and Hadrian, Protus and Hyacinth.

     After Lawr[5]. Cornelius and Cyprian, Nicomede, Euphemia, *Maurice.*

H P Then comes September Embertide, with the Stational Sunday preceding it, and the *Vacat* Sunday following it; and we pause to note how **H** differs from **P** during this half-year. It adds St. Leo on the Vigil of SS. Peter and Paul (June 28); St. Peter ad Vincula (Aug. 1); Vigil of Assumption (Aug. 14). It omits the Passion of John Bapt. at August 29, and Hadrian at September 8. It adds the Exaltation of

H. Cross [a] to September 14; and Lucy and Geminian on September 16. It omits Maurice at September 22.

From this point onward to Christmas there is no variation in the two lists. **H** has in a single block the series Cosmas and Damian to Andrew. The distribution of the days in **P** is as follows:

P After Embertide; Cosmas and Damian, Michaelmas.
After Angeli[1] Mark. After Ang[2].; Callistus.
After Ang[345]. Caesarius.
After Ang[6]. Four Crowned Martyrs, Theodore, Mennas, Martin.
After Ang[78]. Cecilia, Clement, Felicitas, Chrysogonus.
After Ang[9]. Saturninus, Vigil, Andrew.

H P After Advent[2] Lucy.

It is evident that the divergences are few. **P** seems to exhibit an earlier form of Gregorian Kalendar, which lacks Gregory, George, St. Peter's Chains, Vigil of Assumption, Lucy and Geminian; which, with the Nativity of the B.V.M., has retained Hadrian (title only), omitted in **H**; which has the Invention, but not the Exaltation, of Holy Cross; which has also adopted the Passion of St. John Baptist, and, as a local addition, Maurice.

It seems also that the Gregorian book, on which **P** was based, had not the Annunciation; for **P**, like other MSS. of this mixed type, puts it in its Gelasian and not its Gregorian position. Probably also it had not the Assumption or the Nativity, for the Masses provided are Gelasian, not Gregorian.[b] It had not adopted the Thursdays in Lent, for **P** mentions them defectively and wrongly.[c] In fact

---

[a] **P** has only a single Collect, *ad crucem salutandam in S. Petro.*

[b] Apart from this the Saints-days common to both books have the same Masses except perhaps St. Felix (Jan. 16).

[c] Also the masses differ from **H**; see Andrieu in *Revue des Sciences Religieuses,* 35 (July 1929) pp. 343 & ff.

we have worked back to a Gregorian Sacramentary of the 7th century.

In other Mixed Sacramentaries (such as S, A, and G) the Kalendar exhibits a more extensive adoption of Gelasian days. The Gregorian Kalendar which lies behind them as groundwork seems to represent a stage intermediate between the Gregorian groundwork of **P** and the Kalendar of **H**; for it has Gregory, George, Vigil of Assumption, Exaltation of H. Cross, and the addition of SS. Lucy and Geminian—agreeing thereby with **H**; but it does not contain the other two days which **H** has and **P** has not, viz. Leo and St. Peter's Chains.

On the Gelasian side also this group of Mixed Sacramentaries represents a more developed stage than **P**, for they contain all **P**'s Gelasian days (except Maurice), and many more.

The distribution of the Saints-days follows the same general plan as in **P**, but the details vary after Pentecost. S has not, like **P**, the plan of reckoning the Sundays in groups, five after Pentecost, six after Apostles, five after Lawrence, two at Embertide, nine after Michaelmas—twenty-seven in all, besides four in Advent. Instead of this S, A, R add an extra Sunday after Pent[3]. and so reckon twenty-seven Sundays after Pentecost as well as a 5th Sunday before Christmas, before reaching the usual four Sundays in Advent. This additional Sunday involves no rearrangement in the distribution of the Saints-days;[a] and there is none except to a very slight degree in Pent[13-15]. The Gellonense (G) agrees in distribution almost entirely with these, allowing for the fact that it has one Sunday less, and reckons Pent[27]. as the equivalent of the 5th before Christmas, and so on; thus arriving at a total of thirty-two Sundays after Pentecost before Christmas.

[a] The added entry of St. Maurice shows its lateness by figuring in differing places in the distribution.

It is evident that here is a group of Mixed Sacramentaries, which, while differing in detail, are based upon a common plan and have a common origin.

S is the best representative of this class and the best known.[a] So far as the contents of the *Sanctorale* are concerned, we note the following additions to the list given above representing **P** and **H**.

After Theoph[2]. SS. *Marius and Martha* (Jan. 19).
After Theoph[3]. SS. Emerentiana and Macarius (Jan. 23).
 St. Praejectus, and Conversion of St. Paul (Jan. 25).
After Theoph[5]. *St. Sotheris* and SS. Zoticus Irenaeus and Hyacinth (Feb. 10).
After Theoph[6]. add to February 14. *Vitalis, Felicula, and Zeno.*
 St. Juliana (Feb. 16).
 Cathedra Petri (Feb. 22).
 SS. Perpetua and Felicitas (Mar. 7).
After Oct. Pasch. St. Leo (Apr. 11).
 St. Euphemia (Apr. 13).
After Oct. Pasch[3]. add to May 3 *St. Juvenal*, and *Invention of H. Cross.*[b]
After Pent[2]. SS. Primus and Felician (June 9).
 SS. Basilides *Cyrinus Nabor and Nazarius* (June 12).
After Pent[4]. *St. Vitus* (June 15).
 Add to June 18 the Vigil of SS. Gervasius and Protasius.
After Pent[5]. *Vigil of SS. John and Paul* (June 25).
After Pent[8]. St. Benedict (July 11).
After Pent[10]. St. James (July 25).
 SS. Simplicius Faustinus and Beatrice (July 28 not 29)
After Pent[11]. *Machabees* (Aug. 1).
 St. Donatus (Aug. 7).

---

[a] The outline is given in Wilson's *Gelasian*: it is printed in full by Mohlberg; and the Gelasian column in the Triplex Sacramentary is almost identical.

[b] After Oct. Pasch[4]. observe Gordian without Epimachus on 10th: Nereus and Achilles as well as Pancras on 12th May.

After Pent[13]. *Oct. of St. Lawrence* (Aug. 17).
  St. Magnus (Aug. 19).
After Pent[14]. St. Bartholomew (Aug. 24).
  St. Rufus (Aug. 27).
After Pent[15]. add to August 29 *Passion of St. John
    Baptist.*
  St. Priscus (Sept. 1).
After Pent[16]. *St. Gorgonius* (Sept. 9).
After Pent[17]. add to September 14 *Exaltation of H.
    Cross* (in **H**, not in **P**), and a special Mass of
    St. Cyprian alone.
After Pent[18]. Vigil and Day of St. Matthew (Sept.
    20 and 21).
After Pent[20]. add to October 7 *SS. Marcellus and
    Apuleius.*
After Pent[22]. St. Luke (Oct. 18).
After Pent[23]. Vigil and Day of SS. Simon and Jude
    (Oct. 27 and 28).
After Pent[26]. St. Augustine (Nov. 16).
After Pent[27]. *Vigil of St. Cecilia* (Nov. 21).
After Dom. V. ante Natale; add on November 29 with
    St. Saturninus also *SS. Chrysanthus Maurus and
    Daria.*
After Dom. IV; *Octave of St. Andrew* (Dec. 7).
  St. Damasus (Dec. 11).
After Dom. *vacat*; St. Thomas (Dec. 21).

The greater part of these entries have already been
observed as characteristic of the Early Gelasian **V** (above
p. 40). The rest require some explanation. The entries
which are most clearly Frankish, and therefore may be
presumed to have been added to the Gelasian tradition
after it left Italy, are these: St. Praejectus the martyred
bishop of Clermont in the Auvergne[a] (*c.* 670) on
January 25. St. Benedict on July 11, the date of the

---

[a] *Ephemerides Liturg.* xliii (1929), pp. 93–9.

E

translation to Fleury on the Loire (653). Possibly the Macarius on January 23 is an Angevin Abbot of the 5th century.[a]

Many of the entries are due to a desire to commemorate Apostles which seems to have arisen at this era in France.[b] Thus the Conversion of St. Paul is balanced by the Chair of St. Peter. Besides we note the addition of St. James, St. Bartholomew, St. Matthew, St. Luke, SS. Simon and Jude, St. Thomas, to fill out the list of Apostles and Evangelists.

Others, however, look back to Rome, especially the addition of SS. Primus and Felician on June 9 and St. Basilides on June 12. Both these days belong to the early Gregorian tradition, as the Lectionaries will show (p. 71). Their presence here shows that the Gregorian substratum of this group differed in this respect from what underlay **H** or **P**. There is, however, no early Gregorian evidence as yet for St. Emerentiana on January 23, SS. Zoticus Irenaeus and Hyacinth[c] on February 10; St. Zeno[d] added on February 14; St. Leo on April 11, not on June 28 as in **H**; St. Damasus on December 11; though these are all of them Roman saints. It would seem that they were added to the Kalendar in France; and there is a parallel to this in the case of the Old Roman Martyrology, for that, too, incorporated additional Roman saints after it came to France.

The remaining entry takes us back to Capua, for the St. Augustine set down between St. Martin and St. Cecilia as xv. Kal. Nov. must be meant for xvi. Kal. Dec. = Nov. 16, the date of the Capuan commemoration of SS. Augustine and Felicitas.[e] This is not in **V**, nor is it in the Old English Martyrology with the other

---

[a] Hollweck, *Biog. Dict. of the SS.* (1924).

[b] The same feature is noticeable in England on comparing Bede's Martyrology (*c.* 731) with the Pseudo-Bede's poetical Kalendar. See Quentin, *Mart. Historiques* (Paris, 1908), pp. 115 ff., 126 ff.

[c] K. 137–9.   [d] K. 207.   [e] Lanzoni, 190 ff.

Capuan entries; but it is in Willibrord's Kalendar, as *In Capua Augustini et Felicitatis*, which corresponds with the Epternach family of MSS. of the Early Roman Martyrology. Evidently to a later generation the entry must have caused trouble. It must probably have come into the Mixed Sacramentaries through an English channel.[a] It was probably retained out of respect for the name of St. Augustine, while other Capuan entries figuring in the source were omitted. But in other Sacramentaries of this group—Gellone,[b] and Angoulême, as in Fulda—St. Augustine appears on the usual date, August 28.

The Kalendar in other Mixed Sacramentaries of this group is very similar. Gellone, for example, is substantially the same, though it omits the Conversion of St. Paul, has a Mass of another Marcellus, martyr, at January 17; adds St. Jerome, September 30; and has incorporated the peculiar '*Missa prohibendo ab idolis*' like V at January 1.

Angoulême again is similar; but has added various local feasts, including (like S) St. Maurice, and also a dedication festival of St. Martin at Tours. Phillips adds a number of Frankish saints. The Palimpsest fragment from an Angelica MS. has Felicitas at August 1.

The Fulda Sacramentary, both in the Kalendar and in the arrangement, shows a later development, but points back to a similar origin.

The groundwork of this group is again, as in the case of **P**, a form of Gregorian Sacramentary, but earlier and more normal than that of **P**.

The further interrelation of these three types—Gelasian, Gregorian, and Mixed—is an alluring topic; but this is not the place to pursue it. We have amassed

---

[a] Perhaps another relic of the Capuan tradition was the observance at Canterbury of November 16 as the Ordination of St. Augustine *of Canterbury*.

[b] As presbyter: and the Capuan saint is properly a local martyr and not the African bishop. See Lanzoni, 196.

data from them for our immediate purpose, the study of the Kalendar, and we must now pass on to the Lectionaries.

x. *The Lectionaries*

Turning to the early Lectionaries we find much light thrown by them on the earlier Gregorian tradition. The four documents already used in studying the Stations (p. 17) carry us back to the same era as that of the early Gelasian, i.e. the beginning of the 8th century, or earlier. The Würzburg Epistle-list **We**, like most books if its class, deals very cavalierly with the *Sanctorale*. It is evidence for what it contains; but a negative argument must not be built upon it. The four Gospel-lists —**Wg, Jon, Qr**, and **R**—agree almost entirely as to the *Sanctorale*, and are presumably full lists.[a] The guiding feature as to date is the absence of the Thursdays in Lent instituted by Gregory II (715–31), and the days included are therefore those observed at the entrance to the 8th century.[b]

They are set out on the same plan as **P** and the later Mixed Sacramentaries, that is to say the Saints-days are intercalated among the Sundays, as well as those ferias which are, in Lectionaries, associated with the Sundays. The details of arrangement and distribution necessarily differ; for in those early days to which the Lectionary-lists belong there were reckoned to be ten Sundays after *Theophania*, and only twenty after Pentecost. This

[a] MS. Mp. Th. fol. 62 of the University of Würzburg contains the two lists. See *Revue Bénéd.* xxvii. 41, and xxviii. 296. The Reims Gospel-book is MS. 10 at Rheims. **Jon** is Vatican MS. Pal. Latin 46. (Cp. p. 17).

[b] Morin dated **Wg** half a century later because it contains the festival of SS. Primus and Felician (June 9), of St. Euplius (Aug. 12). It is true that it was Theodore (642–9) who translated these Saints to St. Stephen's, and that he built an Oratory for St. Euplius. But it is surer ground to argue from the Lenten Thursdays than from these Saints-days. The cult of St. Euplius may easily have preceded the erection of the Oratory: and the cult of these martyrs began at their tomb before translation. It seems even to have waned after the translation, for the day is not in **P** or **H**.

difference naturally affects the details of the spacing in those two seasons. In Eastertide, where there is no difference between the Sacramentaries and the Lectionaries as to the number of Sundays, the spacing is similar, but not identical.

The Würzburg Epistle-list is early and interesting, but it contributes little to our inquiry into the Kalendar. Very few Saints-days are mentioned as having proper lessons—only Stephen, John Evang., H. Innocents, Sebastian, Agnes, Agatha: there are none in Eastertide: then follow Philip and James, John Baptist, John and Paul, Peter, Paul, Sixtus, Lawrence, Sabina, Michaelmas, Andrew—and these not in strict kalendrical order. The list for Sundays is almost equally unsatisfying.

The Sundays are Nativ.[1-4], LXX, LX, L, XL,[a] Tricesima, Ante Vicesima, In Mediana, Indulgentia,[3] Pasch., Oct. Pasch., Oct. Pasch.[1-9], Pent., In Natale Sanctorum (Pent[1].), covering the first half-year; for the second half there is nothing except five Sundays of Advent.

The only ferias mentioned are: (*a*) those of Lent (excluding the Thursdays, Lvii and XL[5]vii), Easter Week, Litania Maior, Vig. Pent.; (*b*) the Ember days in Lent, in the week following the Sunday in Natale Sanctorum, in the week following St. Lawrence, and in the week following St. Andrew and preceding Advent [1]; (*c*) the Vigils of Christmas, St. John Baptist, St. Peter, St. Paul, St. Lawrence, St. Andrew; (*d*) four lessons post Theophania. The separate Vigil of St. Paul seems to point to Rome, the place where it was most natural to perform a Vigil-service on the evening of June 29 and to keep the services of St. Peter and St. Paul separate from one another. It is possible that the entry preceding that of SS. John and Paul is to be taken as referring to a vigil, and therefore points the same way, although hitherto we have encountered such a vigil as a Gelasian feature. The

[a] The *Vacat* Sunday, XL[2], is unmentioned.

entry of the Dedication in November may perhaps corroborate the point, if it may be referred to November 18 which was, at any rate in later days, kept as the Dedicatio basilicarum Apostolorum Petri et Pauli.[a]

But the most noteworthy feature of **We** for our present purpose is the way in which, like the *Leonianum*, it seems to group alternatives under some leading headings, and so to form at intervals a sort of *Commune Sanctorum*. For example, some alternatives follow St. Silvester, some headed *in Natale Sacerdotum*; others follow 'SS. Agnes and Agatha'. Besides SS. Philip and James follows St. Paul, being attracted thither out of its proper place. In all 176 entries out of 255 have a definite place assigned to them in the year. The rest from No. 177 onward are less orderly arranged. Down to No. 213 they are mainly for Votive Masses, including Ordination and Matrimony. But among them is an entry of St. Sabina, another for Dedication, and a fresh 'common' group of five *in Natale Sanctorum*. The remaining forty-two are unallotted, being extracts from the 'Pauline' Epistles,[b] given in their biblical order.

With this Epistle-list we seem to be at an early stage of the Kalendar; but such lists, down to much later days, keep an archaic form, so it is not very safe to lay much stress upon the point.

The Gospel-lists are much less peculiar, for in their general line they are not markedly unlike the Sacramentaries. The chief point of distinction in them is that they carry us better backward to the earlier stages of the Gregorian tradition.

This Gregorian list of *c.* 700 deserves to be set out in full, as derived from **Wg** and **R**:

Dec.	Dec.
26. Stephen.	28. Innocents.
27. John Evang.	31. Silvester.

[a] Vatican Antiphonal in Tommasi, *Opp.* iv.
[b] One of these has the heading 'In adventu judicum'.

Jan.
14. Felix in Pincis.
16. Marcellus.
18. Prisca.
20. Sebastian.
    Fabian.
21. Agnes de passione.
22. Vincent.
28. Agnes de nativitate.
Feb.
 2. Purification.[a]
 5. Agatha.
14. Valentine.
April
14. Tiburtius, Valerian, and
    Maximus.
25. Litania maior.
28. Vitalis.
May
 1. Philip and James.
 3. Alexander, Eventius, [and
    Theodolus [b]].
10. Gordian.
12. Nereus and Achilles.
    Pancras.
13. Dedic. S. Marie ad martyres.[c]
19. Pudentiana.[d]
June
 2. Marcellinus and Peter.[e]
 9. Primus and Felician.
12. Basilides.[f]
18. Mark and Marcellian.
19. Gervasius and Protasius.
23. Vigil.
24. John Baptist.
26. John and Paul.
28. Vigil of Peter and Paul.
29. Peter and Paul.
30. Paul.
July
 2. Processus and Martinian.

July.
 6. Oct. Apostolorum.
10. Septem Fratres.
21. Praxedis.[e]
23. Apollinaris.
28. Felix, Simplicius, Faustinus,
    and Beatrice.[g]
30. Abdon and Sennen.
Aug.
 2. Pope Stephen.
 6. Sixtus, Felicissimus, and Ag.
 8. Cyriac.
 9. Vigil.
10. Lawrence.
11. Tiburtius.
12. Euplius.[b]
13. Hippolytus.
14. Eusebius.
15. Nat. S. Mariae **Wg**: Sollemnia
    S. Mariae **R, Jon**.
18. Agapitus.
22. Timothy [and Symphorian **R,
    Jon**].
28. Hermes.
29. Sabina.
30. Felix and Adauctus [Deposi-
    tion of Elisha and Decoll.
    of John Bapt. **R, Jon**].
Sept.
 8. Hadrian.
11. Protus and Hyacinth.
14. Cornelius [and Cyprian **R, Jon**].
15. Nicomede.
16. Lucy and Euphemia.
26. Cosmas and Damian.
29. Dedic. eccl. S. Angeli.
Oct.
 7. Mark.
14. Callistus.[h]
Nov.
 1. Caesarius.

[a] Set out of place at the end of month in **Wg**. [b] Not in **R, Jon**.
[c] Not in **Wg**. In **R, Jon** without any Gospel. [d] Has no Gospel.
[e] Misplaced in **Wg**. [f] Without any Gospel in **Wg**, **Jon**: not found in **R**.
[g] Faustinus Felix and Beatrice in **R, Jon**. [h] Not in **Jon**.

Nov.	Nov.
8. Four Crowned Martyrs.	23. Felicitas.
9. Theodore.	24. Chrysogonus.
11. Mennas.	29. Saturninus, Vigil.
12. Martin.	30. Andrew.[a]
22. Cecilia.	Dec.
23. Clement.	13. Lucy.

It is noticeable that neither the Annunciation nor the Nativity is found here; and the Purification in **Wg** is an afterthought. The Assumption is as yet the only one of the four great Marian days that has a solid position. Other feasts found in **P**, and **H**, but not here, are these:

In **P**, *not in* **H**.	*In both* **H** *and* **P**.	*In* **H**, *not in* **P**.
May 3. Inv. of Holy Cross.	May 6. John Port-Latin.	March 12. Gregory.
[Aug. 30. Decollation]	25. Urban.	May 10. add Epimachus.
	June 1. Nicomede.	April 23. George.
		June 28. Leo.
		Aug. 1. St. Peter ad Vincula.
		14. Vig. of Assumption.
		Sept. 14. Exalt. of H. Cross.
		16. Lucy and Geminian.

On the other hand it has, and **P, H**, have not, the following:

May 12. Nereus and Achilles.
    19. Pudentiana (but without Gospel in **R**).
June 9. Primus and Felician.
    12. Basilides (without Gospel and in **Wg** only).
July 21. Praxedis.
    23. Apollinaris.
Aug. 12. Euplius (**Wg** only).
    30. Add Elisha.
Sept. 16. Add Lucy.

[a] The last two are not in **Wg** because it is incomplete.

We seem to see three forms of addition to this Kalendar which have taken place in the 8th century:

(*a*) From a Gelasian source—The Purification, Annunciation, and Nativity, Invention of Holy Cross, Decollation of St. John Baptist. For all these are found in the more or less contemporary Gelasian MS. **V**.

(*b*) Earlier Gregorian additions—St. John Port-Latin, Urban, and Nicomede.

(*c*) Later Gregorian additions—Gregory, George, Leo (June 28), St. Peter ad Vincula, Vigil of Assumption, Exalt. of H. Cross, Lucy and Geminian.[a]

So far as the additions are concerned, which are found here but not in the Sacramentaries, they are all of Roman origin, unless it be the intercalation of Elisha on August 30. We thus are brought back by the Lectionaries to an early Gregorian tradition that lies far behind the *Hadrianum*; but it is not the same as the form of that tradition which lies behind the Sacramentaries.

When we come to the 8th century, the middle and latter part, we observe that the Carolingian Lectionaries have behind them a different form of Gregorian again. They are principally of two types, one more closely allied than the other to the above-mentioned tradition. The most widespread type—to judge by the number of MSS. extant now—is the more closely allied. It adds Gregory, Annunciation, George, Urban, Felicula, Cyriac, St. Peter ad Vincula, Susanna,[b] Genesius, Nativity B.V.M., Exaltation of H. Cross, Eustace, Chrysanthus and Daria; that is to say, it approximates to the Sacramentaries **H, P**. This may be called the 'standard' type.

[a] The Translation of St. Leo was effected by Sergius (687–701): and he also was concerned with the incorporation of the Holy Cross Day in September. *L. P.* i. 374–6.

[b] The incorporation of Susanna is perhaps also the result of the influence of Sergius; for he was priest of that *titulus*, and adorned and enriched it. Ibid., 379, 380.

The second Carolingian type of Lectionary, one which seems to have been specially distributed from Aachen, has further additions to the *Sanctorale* among its distinguishing features, especially St. Martina on January 1 and the Translation of St. Leo on June 28. It lacks some of the Saints-days which found a temporary or insecure place in the other type, e.g. Felicula, Susanna, Genesius. It may be called the 'Martina type'.[a]

All these variant *Sanctoralia*, and others too of less popularity than these, are the result not of alterations made outside Italy in their adopted land but in the homeland; they represent variant stages or types of native Gregorian Kalendar.

The Lectionaries have much less light to throw on the Gelasian tradition. The Lindisfarne Lectionary is not essentially Roman at all, but Capuan; and the Burchard Lectionary (*c.* 740)[b] is a combination of the Northumbrian list with a form of Gregorian which includes St. Gregory, but not the Lenten Thursdays. There is no known Lectionary which corresponds with the Gelasian Sacramentary **V**. There are, however, some 'Mixed' Lectionaries. The best representative of this group is Athelstan's G. Book, which follows **V** in arranging the Saints-days separately as *De nataliciis sanctorum* and has the following familiar Gelasian entries.[c]

Jan. 23. Emerentiana and Macarius.
Feb. 10. Zoticus Irenaeus and Hyacinth.
    14. With Valentine are Vitalis Felicula and Zeno.
    22. Cathedra Petri.
Apr. 11. Leo.

[a] Her church, built on the ruins of part of the Senate House is not attested earlier than Hadrian's time (772–95). Huelsen, 381.

[b] *Rev. Bénéd.* x (1893), 113 ff.

[c] Brit. Museum MS. Tiberius A. 2. Compare the Murbach Lectionary in *Rev. Bénéd.* xxx (1913), p. 35: Paris Bibl. Nat. Latin MS. 262, and others.

May 3. Invention of H. Cross.
June 13. Add Cyrinus Nabor and Nazarius.
July 29. Add Simplicius Faustinus and Beatrice.
Aug. 1. Machabees.
    19. Magnus.
    27. Rufus.
    29. Passio Joh. Bapt.
Sept. 14. Exalt. H. Cross.

With these French lists may be placed an Italian list which exhibits Gelasian additions of a different sort.[a]

Feb. 14. Vitalis (of Spoleto).
    17. Felix.[b]
May 4. Invention of H. Cross.
   6. Natale S. Johannis Euang.[c]
June 13. Add Nabor and Nazarius.
Aug. 7. Donatus.
    22. Add Symphorian.
Sept. 9. Gorgonius.

From the evidence, so far as it is available, it would appear that there were not two 'Roman' types of Lectionary, one Gelasian and the other Gregorian, as is the case with the Sacramentaries. But that some Lectionaries were influenced in respect of their *Sanctorale* by the Gelasian Mass-books. There is, however, a noteworthy series of ferial Gospels to be found in the Lectionaries which exhibits signs of Gelasian influence. This series is mainly supplementary, but partly also alternative, to the corresponding set in the Standard Gregorian Lectionaries. It may possibly be considered as 'Gelasian', but its influence is found in many capitularies which are uninfluenced by Gelasian Saints-days.[d]

[a] Vatican MS. Barberini Latin 637.
[b] Is this the saint found in the Monza Gradual next after St. Valentine?
[c] This is a marginal addition. The observance of two days connected with St. John Evang. is as early as the Capuan list, and Murbach Capitulary.
[d] The further problems presented by the Lectionaries will be treated in a later Essay.

The main contribution then of the Lectionaries is the early evidence that they afford as to the contents of the Gregorian *Sanctorale* within a century after St. Gregory's death.

xi. *The Choir-books*

There remains the evidence of the music-books to be taken into account. This for various reasons is different from the rest. If other books developed independently of one another, the books of the singers did so especially. Any provision of new music is made with much more difficulty than either the addition of a new set of Collects, &c., forming a 'Mass' for the celebrant, or the addition of fresh Epistles and Gospels. If the composer is moved to write a new office, all well and good; if not, the musical portions must be borrowed entire from elsewhere, or existing music must be adapted to new words. In fact both these methods were followed both for the Mass and for the Office; but much more extensively in the latter than in the former. The procedure in recording the music of Saints-days is found to have been different in the two music-books, so far as the earliest MSS. reveal them. In the earliest Graduals each day has its own music whether original or borrowed; there is no 'Common of Saints', consequently the *Sanctorale* provides a complete list of the Saints-days contemplated. In the Antiphonal there is a Common of Saints to which the singers must go when there is no special music provided; the *Sanctorale* gives only the special music. So, unless there is a Kalendar or some list, it is not possible to know the complete schedule of the saints whose festivals were observed. The earlier MS. Antiphonals have, in fact, no such Kalendar or list.

Consequently the evidence available for the present purpose comes mainly from the Gradual, though the Antiphonal contributes some supplementary points. The evidence of the Gradual is particularly valuable because of the remarkable conservatism with which successive

generations regarded the chants of the Mass. New music
was very sparingly introduced, and mainly was confined
to those new festivals which in the nature of things could
not suitably borrow, in order to satisfy the need, such
as the Holy Cross days, the Purification, the Assumption.

The Roman chant played the chief part in the
popularizing and diffusion of the Roman rite in Carolingian times. The various forms of native Gallican Sacramentary or Lectionary could put up some fight against
the pervasive Roman Sacramentary or Lectionary. But
there seems to have been no body of Gallican chant in
any form capable of rivalry with the Roman chant. The
chief early requests made to Rome are for the music; the
chief propagators of the Roman rite, whether in England [a]
or in the Frankish Empire, were the singers. Pippin's
first move in the middle of the 8th century envisaged the
chant; for it was the singing of the choir of Pope
Stephen III (752–7) during his visit to France that set the
fashion. Charlemagne followed suit, but with more eye
to the rite; and later on in the contest between Gelasian
and Gregorian the music was on the side of the latter.
No doubt some Gallican music survived and ultimately
gained a place in the 'Mixed' repertory; but this took
place much more in connexion with supplementary
services [b] than with the Mass itself.

The earliest available Gradual (Pam) implies a Kalendar, which is later than the Gospel-books above-mentioned, but earlier than the **H** Sacramentary sent by
Hadrian between 784 and 791. It runs very closely
parallel to the Gospel-books; and the agreement thus
exhibited goes some way to make up for the lack of any
sacramentary of the Gregorian type dating from the early
or middle of the 8th century. But it represents a later

---

[a] The process goes on in England throughout the 7th century. Bede, *H. E.* i.
25; ii. 16, 20; iv. 2, 10, 16; v. 10. *Hist. Abbatum*, 3, 10.
[b] E.g. The Reproaches.

stage of Gregorian, as is evident at once from the inclusion of the Lenten Thursdays. Two other Graduals which may belong to the 8th century, Monza and Rheinau, give too few entries in the *Sanctorale* to be of value for this inquiry. We depend therefore mainly upon Pam, which has a *Sanctorale* like that given above (pp. 70 ff.) from the earliest Gospel-lists, together with the following additions, and some omissions, which may, or may not, be significant.

Added.	*Omitted.*
Mar. 12. Gregory.	
25. Annunciation.	
Apr. 23. George.	
May 3. Prefix Juvenal.[a]	
	May 12. Nereus and Achilles.
25. Urban.	
	July 28. (Felix).
	Aug. 12. Euplius.
Aug. 17. Octave of Lawrence.	
Sept. 20, 21. St. Matthew and Vigil.	
	Oct. 14. Callistus.
Oct. 27 28. SS. Simon and Jude, with Vigil.	
	Nov. 12. Martin.
	23. Felicitas.
	24. Chrysogonus.
	29. Saturninus.

It remained for the Carolingian Graduals to make good the omissions (except Euplius, whose days were over), to add the two festivals of Holy Cross, and Gorgonius. But

---

[a] This is perhaps a Gelasian touch. Cp. Chartres Gradual.

there still remain some feasts of the *Hadrianum* un-
adopted, such as St. John Port-Latin, the Dedic. of St.
Nicomede, St. Leo (June 28), the Nativity of the
B.V.M. These data agree largely with the development observed above in the Gospel-books; and the agreement is all the more notable because the Graduals are
very independent in other respects. They habitually
begin with the First Sunday in Advent; their scheme of
arrangement is partly a fusion of *Temporale* and *Sanctorale*, and partly not. Ordinarily it proceeds thus.

They put St. Lucy in Advent and the usual Saints-days
in Christmastide. After Epiphany there are only three
Sundays provided, and these follow January 6, 14, 21.
The Sundays after Easter are grouped to follow Low
Sunday; one Sunday follows Ascension Day; and the
Sundays after Oct. Pent., twenty-three in number, come
last on the list.

But there is another scheme represented by the
Rheinau Gradual. This begins with the fifth Sunday
before Christmas, has four Sundays after Theoph. all
grouped together to follow the day. Four Sundays follow
Low Sunday; one follows Ascension Day; five follow Oct.
Pent. Then comes St. John Baptist. Oct. Pent[6-12]. follow,
and a gap in the MS. occurs in the last of these. The
MS. begins again in the latter part of Michaelmas,
which is followed by Oct. Pent[18-23].

Another sign of independence is the record of Stations
given in the Graduals—especially the fact that at the
beginning in Advent some of them prescribe Stations for
the Sundays. The first Sunday, indeed, may have none,
being lost perhaps in the glory of the opening initial;
but the second has 'Hierusalem', and the third St.
Peter's. The St. Gall. MS. 359, however, devotes a page
to recording for Adv[1]. *Statio ad S. Andream post praesepe*.[a]

But the chief importance of this music-book is that it

----

[a] See above, p. 22.

makes it possible to get behind the existing form and work back to the state of things for which the music was composed. Many of the compositions are used several times, and the use of them is, in the early books, very fairly uniform;[a] so it is possible to a large extent to distinguish the festivals which borrowed from those which lent, and so to distinguish the later from the earlier.

The *Sanctorale* for which the music was written must have contained at least the following Saints-days:

Dec.
26. Stephen.
27. John Evang.
28. Holy Innocents.
31. Silvester.
Jan.
  1. St. Mary, the Octave of the Lord.
16. Marcellus.
18. Prisca.
21. Agnes.
Feb.
  2. Purification.
  5. Agatha.
14. Valentine*.
Mar.
25. Annunciation.
Apr.
22. Tiburtius and Valerian*.
23. George.
25. Litania maior.
28. Vitalis.

May
  1. Philip and James.
  3. Invention of H. Cross.
12. Pancras.
13. St. Mary ad martyres.
June
  2. Marcellinus and Peter*.
12. Basilides*.
19. Gervasius and Protasius.
23. Vigil.
24. John Baptist.
26. John and Paul.
28. Vigil.
29. Peter and Paul.
30. Paul.
July
  2. Processus and Martinian.
  6. Octave of the Apostles.
10. Septem Fratres.
23. Apollinaris.
29. Felix*.

[a] Except as regards Alleluias: because these, in history and use, stand apart from the rest of the chant. They are therefore of no use for the present purpose, and are not taken into account here.

Aug.
- 6. Sixtus.
- 8. Cyriac.
- 9. Vigil.
- 10. Lawrence (2 Masses).
- 13. Hippolytus.
- 15. Assumption.
- 22. Timothy (and Symplorian).
- 28. Hermes.
- 29. Sabina.
- 30. Felix and Adauctus.

Sept.
- 8. Hadrian*.
- 21. Matthew.

Sept.
- 29. Michaelmas.

Oct.
- 28. Simon and Jude.

Nov.
- 1. Caesarius*.
- 9. Quatuor Coronati*.
- 11. Mennas.
- 22. Cecilia.
- 23. Clement.
- 29. Vigil.
- 30. Andrew.

Dec.
- 13. Lucy.

No doubt it contained more; and, as in some cases it is doubtful which is the borrower, the list is not quite certain.[a] For example, St. Pudentiana has the same music as St. Lucy, so it is possible that her name (at May 19) should be inserted instead of that of Lucy. But the list shows the festivals for which the Roman musicians had to provide, or at any rate did provide. It is noticeable that there is very little which is subsequent to St. Gregory's date; and also that a minimum list extracted from the early Gospel-books would contain mainly the same set of names.

The chief authorities for the early Gradual are the following:
A. Three MSS. seem to go back to the middle of the 8th century.

1. Pam. Brussels MS. 10127–44. The MS. used by Pamelius as basis of his edition (*Liturgicon*, ii. 62. Paris 1571, 1609). It has been described by Dom Peillon in *Revue Bénédictine*, xxix. (Oct. 1912), 411–37. It must be further observed that it is a rough book with hardly a scrap of notation: it degenerates at times into being little but a list of catchwords. It is not purely Roman, for it contains a note to Oct. Pent[7]., *Ista ebdomata non est in ante fonarios Romanos.*

2. The Monza Gradual, printed in Tommasi, *Opp.* v. 257–66. This

[a] The uncertain points are those marked with the asterisk.

F

contains Graduals only with Tracts and Alleluias, and is probably the earliest extant book of the kind. It is said to have been given to Monza by Theodelinda, but it can hardly be so early. The inclusion of SS. Denys and Rusticus points to a Frankish origin, or may be a reminiscence of the visit of Stephen III to Paris (755). The provenance of the book might be settled by identifying the St. Felix who is found between St. Valentine and Septuagesima. He is perhaps the Saint found on February 17 in the Gelasian Capitulary (see p. 75) of Barberini MS. Lat. 637: but it has not been possible to trace him satisfactorily. In any case the *Sanctorale* is not a full one.

3. Rheinau. Gradual Rheinau MS. 30 at Zürich: printed in Gerbert, *Mon. Vet. Lit. Alemann.*, i. 353 ff. For the MS. of the Rheinau Sacramentary (R. above, p. 57) see Wilson, *Gelasian Sacr.*, p. xxxii ff. It suffers from having a very small *Sanctorale*.

B. There is a large group of MSS. similar in character and belonging mainly to the 9th century.

4. St. Gall. MS. 359. A Book of Graduals only, with cues given of the rest of the music. Facsimile by Lambillotte (1851) and again in *Paléogr. Musicale* (2nd series).

5. Gradual of Compiègne. Paris, Bibl. Nat., Fonds Latin 17436, collated in *P. L.*, LXXVIII. 641–724 with the text of Pamelius. The lists of musical cues in two Sacramentaries of St. Thierry [Reims MSS. 213 (9th cent.), and 214 (10th cent.): see Leroquais, nos. 8 and 36], are also collated there.

6. Gradual of Chartres MS 47: see Tommasi, *Opp.*, v. 267–88.

7. Gradual of St. Gall MS. 339 in *Paléogr. Musicale*, i. $x\frac{1}{2}$.

8. Gradual of Einsiedeln in *Paléogr. Musicale*, ii.

9. Gradual of Laon MS. 239 in *Paléogr. Musicale*, x.   ix/x.

10. Sacramentary of Ottobon MS. 313 at the Vatican. A Gregorian Sacramentary (O. p. 52) with cues of the music. See Wilson, *Gregorian Sacr.*, p. xxviii.   ix.

11. Sacramentary of St. Amand: Paris, Bibl. Nat. Fonds Latin 2291, with list of musical cues: printed in Netzer, *Introduction de la Messe Romaine* (Paris 1910), see p. 98 and Appendix: Leroquais 19.   ix/x.

12. Sacramentary of Rodradus from Corbie (Rod. p. 52): Paris Bibl. Nat. Fonds Latin 12050, with a list of musical cues. Collated with the above, see p. 93 and Appendix: Leroquais 9.   *c.* 850.

13. Sacramentary of Senlis: Paris, St. Geneviève MS. BB. 20, with list of musical cues. Collated with the book of St. Amand: see Netzer, p. 96 and Appendix: Leroquais 12.   *c.* 880.

The Antiphonal has much less evidence to bring, because few of the festivals of saints have proper music. The old type of music is found for Stephen, John, Holy Innocents, Paul, Sebastian, Agnes, Agatha, John Baptist, John and Peter and Paul, Commemoration of Paul, Lawrence, Assumption, Michaelmas, Cecilia, Clement, Andrew, Lucy. The music of the Purification, Decollation, Holy Cross, and St. Martin is mainly of later date. Beyond these, except perhaps for Vincent, Conversion of St. Paul, Annunciation, George, Philip and James, there is no music generally provided till Carolingian times.

PART II

IN the preceding Part a good deal of material has been accumulated, which has given some idea of the stages in the growth of the Roman Kalendar. The chief sources of information have been:

(*a*) the Philocalian lists telling what names were honoured in the middle of the 4th century;

(*b*) the Old Roman Martyrology formulated half a century later, enlarged in Italy during the 5th century, transplanted to Gaul in the 6th, and there increased progressively;

(*c*) the lists of *tituli*, *diaconiae*, and Stational churches in Rome beginning at the end of the 5th century, so far as the *tituli* are concerned, and not earlier than the 7th century so far as the Stations go.

(*d*) The Service-books supply: (1) an incomplete list of the middle of the 6th century in the *Leonianum*; (2) a Gelasian list of the end of the 7th century or a little later; (3) Gregorian lists of several kinds, the earliest of which is only slightly later; (4) various fusions of the two made in the 8th and 9th centuries.

(*e*) Ecclesiological data, collected principally from the *Liber Pontificalis*, illustrate and supplement the evidence, because church and cult are very closely connected together.

It now remains to consider the various entries in the Kalendar separately, and in their liturgical order, and to estimate the antiquity of their claim to a place there.

DECEMBER

The year begins with Christmas,[a] which with the three feasts following is found as early as in the Leonine

[a] This is usual with early Sacramentaries and Capitularies, but the *Leonianum* began at January, and the Graduals generally begin at Advent.

Sacramentary. But there the services of the protomartyr have been placed under the entry of Pope Stephen on August 2. Two Masses apiece are provided there for St. John Evangelist and the Holy Innocents.

Dec. 31. One subsequent day in December claims attention. The *Leonianum* has no entry of St. Silvester on December 31; but in Section XXXIV there is a Mass for the Deposition of St. Silvester, Bishop and Confessor, set immediately before November among the services SUPER DEFUNCTOS. Presumably this is another case of transposition, for its proper place would be at December 31 where the deposition is noted in the Philocalian Kalendar. The observance of this day is therefore well rooted in the Roman tradition though Silvester was joined with Martin as patron of the *titulus Equitii*; but the day is not marked in the early Gelasian **V**. The Gradual shows that it had music of its own; and it is entered in **We** the earliest Epistle-book, as well as in the early Gospel-lists. The church of the saint is the old *titulus Equitii*, and the saint is its reputed founder. The Stational Mass was held there on XL⁴v.

JANUARY

The entries of this month that by common agreement of the different sources belong to the old Roman Kalendar are these, in the left-hand column; later additions are in the column on the right hand.

1. Octava domini. Circumcision.	Martina
5. Vigilia Theophaniae.	
6. Theophania.	
14. Felix.	
16. Marcellus.	
	18. Prisca. Cathedra Petri.
20. Sebastian, Fabian.	Marius, Martha, Audifax, and Habacuk.
21. Agnes de passione.	
	22. Vincent.
	23. Emerentiana, Macarius.
	25. Conversion of St. Paul,
28. Agnes de nativitate.	Praejectus.

[A.] Jan. 1. Octave of the Lord. This is the old title of this day in both Gelasian and Gregorian early sources. But it is not clear when the usage began. The principle of an octave was already established at Easter, and very probably there was a practical reason for extending the principle to Christmas. January 1 was the Roman New Year's Day, and as such a day of pagan festival and ceremony. The Church needed to set its own services in rivalry with the heathen observance. The Gelasian has a special Mass on this day headed 'Prohibendum ab Idolis', and this was kept in some of the Mixed Sacramentaries of the 8th century. The conflict of the Church with Idolatry on this day may be traced in a series of Canons belonging to Gaul and Spain down to the 7th century as well as in Christian literature,[a] and the pagan licence of the day died hard.

The title 'Circumcision' comes later. It was inevitable that the Gospel chosen should include Luke ii. 21; but for the Epistle a passage was chosen, Col. i. 25–9, having no reference to circumcision but only to the revelation of the mystery of the Incarnation.[b] Later the Gospel of the day, Luke ii. 21–32, was curtailed by the removal of the verses 22–32 which describe the Purification. These were wanted for February 2 when that feast was established. Then January 1 was left with all the interest of the Gospel concentrated in the Circumcision, and it was natural that that name should become prominent.

In Rome the old name continued;[c] it was the right description of the Mass. But in France the title Circumcision begins to appear in the Carolingian Age, imported probably from the Gallican tradition.[d] It also is found in the Fulda Epistle-list, said to hail from Bishop Victor

---

[a] Kellner, ii, § 17.

[b] This was changed at a later date for a repetition of the Christmas Epistle Tit. iii. 4–7.

[c] It stands alone in the Roman Missal of 1474 (*H. B. S.* i. 29).

[d] See *Missale Gothicum* and *Bobbiense*.

of Capua 541–54.[a] The Station given in early sources is St. Mary ad martyres, which implies a date subsequent to 613; but in many early Gospel-capitularies no Station is given. In later days the Station was transferred to St. Mary in Trastevere.

St. Martina came in when a church dedicated to her was made out of the ruins of the senate House (p. 74).

Jan. 5. The Vigil of the Epiphany like some other vigils forms part of the early Gelasian tradition but not of the early Gregorian. It is not in **H** though it is in all the early Gospel-lists, and in some has St. Peter's assigned to it as Station.

Jan. 14. Felix belonged to Nola, was buried there (3rd century), and his cult at first lay outside Rome. Early in the 6th century Paulinus, the distinguished scholar and writer, a native of southern Gaul, betook himself to Nola, where in his early days he had experienced his first call to Christian life at the tomb of St. Felix. Settling there, first as hermit and later as bishop, he spread the fame of the local saint. The name of Felix is found entered on this day in the Carthaginian Martyrology[b] which dates from the early years of this century. At some unknown date, probably about the same era, a church was built in his honour at Rome on the Pincian hill, called St. Felix in Pincis, in order to distinguish it from the cemeterial church on the *Via Portuensis* belonging to the Roman St. Felix of July 28, 29. It fell into ruin, and was rebuilt by Hadrian (772–95);[c] and this rebuilding is the earliest clear evidence that is extant about the church. The feast is common to early Gelasian and Gregorian; so it may well date back to the 6th century. But it is to be noted that no proper music is provided for it.

[a] *Analecta Maredsolana*, i. 436 ff., or Gerbert, *Monumenta*, i. 409 ff. This has also a mass 'Contra idola'.
[b] Mabillon, *Vetera Analecta*, iii. 398 (1682).   [c] *L. P.* i. 500, 517.

Jan. 16. Marcellus is the Pope (308–9), and his name was very early associated as founder of the old *titulus Marcelli* (or *Romani*). Its earliest mention is in a somewhat fantastical account of the establishment of the *titulus* by Lucina, and of the Pope's death there. This account was inserted in the second edition of the *Liber Pontificalis*.[a] The Station on XL⁵iv was held in this church. Some proper music is provided. All this evidence points to the antiquity of this festival.

Jan. 20. Both Fabian and Sebastian are commemorated according to the Philocalian Kalendar on this day, the former in the cemetery of Callistus, the latter close at hand *ad catacumbas*.[b] Originally a separate observance of each was provided in the Sacramentaries and Gospelbooks. The Gradual, however, provided only one Mass, and that containing nothing proper; while the Antiphonal provided only an office proper to St. Sebastian. The crypt and tomb of St. Sebastian underlay the church now called by his name, but known in early days as the Basilica of the Apostles *ad catacumbas* on the Appian Way. At a much later date when the catacombs were devastated, Eugenius II (824–7) removed the body of the saint. The head was bestowed at the church of the Quatuor Coronati; some bones were given to St. Medard of Soissons, and the rest of the body was taken to St. Peter's at the Vatican, where it remained until it was replaced by Honorius III (1216–27).

On the other hand some relics of St. Fabian (236–50) had been brought from the papal crypt in the cemetery of Callistus, and given the place of honour in the *Basilica ad catacumbas*.[c] This action was doubtless due to the liturgical association of the two saints on January 20, the day common to them, as attested by the Philocalian Kalendar.

---

[a] *L. P.* i. xcix, 164–6.
[b] See Chéramy, *Saint-Sébastien* (Paris, 1925), pp. 22–6.
[c] *L. P.* ii. 74; *J. T. S.* (1926), xxviii, p. 33.

Jan. 21. The martyrdom of St. Agnes is recorded in the Philocalian Kalendar. The liturgical observance of this day is common to early Gregorian and Gelasian. The famous church outside the walls goes back at least to the time of Constantine. There is proper music in the Gradual, and a proper office in the Antiphonal.

Jan. 28. It is not clear at what time the observance of this octave began. There is no sign of it in **We**; and there indeed Agnes and Agatha are set down together on January 21. Otherwise Gelasian and Gregorian agree in having octave as well as feast. The early Gospel-book **Wg** agrees with the Gelasian **V** in distinguishing them as 'the Passion' and 'the Nativity'. The Gregorian Sacramentary only distinguishes the second from the first by adding the word *secundo*. There is no proper music for the Octave.

[B.] Turning now to days which seem to have less ancient authority behind them, we note the feasts of two Roman saints which seem to be later additions. Their position in the order of the Gospel-series varies in different MSS.

Jan. 18. Prisca. The entry is probably derived from the *titulus Priscillae* on the Aventine, which is known from the 5th century onward. It may be connected also with the catacomb of Priscilla on the *Via Salaria*. It is not found in the Early Roman Martyrology,[a] so presumably there is no historic martyr of that name. Probably the feast is the dedication festival of the church; out of it a martyr was developed, and her name, in one or other form, was set in the later recension of the Martyrology. In the 9th century she was identified with the companion of St. Paul;[b] and the *titulus* was called *titulus beatissimorum Aquilae et Priscae*. The entry of Prisca is not found in the early Gelasian **V**; in early

---

[a] Kirsch, 128, 129.   [b] Huelsen, 424.

Gregorian (Gospel-lists of the 7th century) it finds a place sometimes at the end of the second week sometimes at the end of the third week after Epiphany. It has some proper music; but the variation as to the position of the day in the Gospel-books seems to show that it was added to them after they had taken their definite shape.

Jan. 22. Vincent. This case is in several respects like that of Prisca. The entry is not in the Early Roman Martyrology, but is an addition made elsewhere and later. The Carthaginian Martyrology shows that the cult of this Spanish martyr had arisen and spread by the 6th century. It is unknown to the earlier Gelasian **V**. In the early Gregorian Gospel-capitularies[a] the entry is found in two different positions, sometimes in the fourth week after Epiphany, sometimes in the fifth. It has no proper music in the Gradual, but an Office in the Antiphonal. Some books contain the direction *Statio in basilica S. Eusebii*.[b] This evidence seems to show that when the saint's cult was introduced at Rome, there was no church there dedicated to him; and that consequently the service took place on this day in the *titulus* of St. Eusebius[c] as the Stational Mass did on XL⁴vi and Epiph². There seems to have been a suburban monastery of St. Vincent situated *ad Aquas Salvias* just outside the Ostian Gate, which was already in existence when Honorius (625–38) translated thither the head of St. Anastasius.[d] The result of this was the introduction of St. Anastasius also on this day; but this addition is not apparent in the Gregorian Gospel-books till later.

The feast therefore seems to have come in during the 6th century, and independently of any church dedicated to the saint.

[a] It is not in **We,** the Epistle-book.

[b] Amc. Walt.; and, adding *juxta merulana,* **Jon** Rd.

[c] Where already perhaps there was another Vincent in possession. Huelsen, 251.

[d] Kehr, *Registr. Pont. Rom., Italia Pont.* i. 171.

[C.] Next some Gelasian entries are to be noted.

Jan. 20. The Roman martyrs Marius and Martha with their children, Audifax and Habacuk, who figure in the Early Roman Martyrology, are found in the Gelasian, but not in the Gregorian, tradition. Such is the position in **V.** The Mixed Sacramentaries have usually only the parents, and set them on January 19.

Jan. 23. The Mixed Sacramentaries have a Mass of St. Emerentiana[a] and St. Macarius. The former is a Roman martyr buried in the Ostian cemetery, where a chapel testifies to her fame. The latter is perhaps the Angevin Abbot of Mauges belonging to the 5th century.[b] The Roman date of St. Emerentiana is September 16; but the festival was perhaps set at January 23 because of the saint's close connexion with St. Agnes. It is so placed in Bede's Martyrology, and the Old English Martyrology.

Jan. 25. Praejectus comes into the Mixed Sacramentaries and into some Gospel-books; and the entry survived, though overshadowed before long by the Conversion of St. Paul.

Jan. 18, 25. The Gallican church from the 5th century onward[c] kept in January a feast of St. Peter on the 18th, and a feast of St. Paul just a week later on the 25th. The former appears among the Gallican additions to the Roman martyrology as *Cathedra Petri in Roma* or *Dedicatio cathedrae S. Petri apostoli qua primo Romae petrus apostulus sedit.* The liturgical observance of this day in Gaul is clear from the Bobbio Sacramentary, the *Missale Gothicum*, the Lectionary of Luxeuil—both of the 7th century—and from the Kalendar of the Gellone Sacramentary, where the entry runs *secundum Gallos Cathedra S. Petri.* The martyrological entry is due to the liturgical observance.[d] This Gallican feast did not

---

[a] Kirsch, 81, 184; Marucchi, 272.   [b] Hollweck, 631.
[c] See Kirsch in *Jahrb. für Lit.* (1925), v. 48–67.
[d] This is all the more clear because the old Gallican feast of St. Mary, which

survive, and the reason of its disappearance will appear below.

The feast of St. Paul on the 25th is found in the *Missale Gothicum,* and in the Mixed Sacramentaries as *Conversio S. Pauli (in Damasco),* or *Translatio S. Pauli* in early Kalendars. This accounts for the similar martyrological entry added to the Roman Martyrology. The two phrases are identical in meaning; *translatio* does not refer to any translation of relics, but to a change of mind, and is thus a synonym for *conversio.* Rome knew nothing of this feast until it borrowed it from Gallican sources.

FEBRUARY

2. Purification, or Hypapanti, or
    Candlemas.
5. Agatha.
    10. Soteris; Zoticus, Irenaeus, and
        Hyacinth.
14. Valentine.
    14. Vitalis & Felicula; Zeno.
    17. Juliana.
    22. Cathedra Petri.

[A.] Feb. 2. The Purification is the first entry to be considered here. It is deeper rooted in the early Gelasian than in Gregorian tradition. **V** has it under this name; and has as well the three other festivals of the B.V. Mary —the Annunciation (Mar. 25), the Assumption (Aug. 15), and the Nativity (Sept. 8). The Gregorian tradition is much less definite. The Purification is not in **We** (Epistle-book). In **Wg** it is inserted out of place, evidently as an afterthought, on a space that either had been blank before Septuagesima, or else was made by erasing the heading of that section. No name is given, only the date and the Gospel; and this absence of name is found in other Gospel-books.[a] It is more normal to find, as in **R,**

is associated with the *Cathedra* on this day in both Sacramentary and Lectionary is found also in the Martyrology.

[a] See Ra, Hc, MT, and compare the Reichenau Palimpsest Sacramentary, which has the entry twice.

the name *Purificatio S. Mariae*, and two Gospels provided. In the *Hadrianum* and its followers the Greek
name *Ύpapanti* is the one used. This is also characteristic
of most of the Gospel-books of the Martina type. In
some of the Mixed Sacramentaries and Graduals it is
'S. Simeonis'.

The music in the Gradual borrows the Introit from
Trin[8]; the rest is proper. The Office in the Antiphonal
to a large extent uses old themes, but handles them
clumsily, and so betrays that its date lies in the silver age.

The early Gregorian tradition knows only two of the
four feasts of the B.V. Mary which are found in early
Gelasian **V**—this one and the festival of August 15, later
called the 'Assumption'. Apparently these two were first
borrowed from the Gelasian; the Nativity next, and the
Annunciation last.

This is the only place at which in the Service-books the
direction for the *collecta* and procession has survived[a]
either in the form, *Oratio ad collectam ad S. Adrianum*
in the **H** book, or *Collecta ad S. Adrianum* in the Mixed
Sacramentaries. But, in fact, the assembly was being made
on all the four days by this date; and, indeed, the collect
is provided for the purpose in **H**. This association of a
procession with the festivals of the B.V.M. must be later
in origin than the time of Honorius (625–38) who
changed the old Senate-house into St. Hadrian's. It
probably arose when the feast of the Nativity was adopted,
for it fell on September 8, a day already kept at St.
Hadrian's. It seems as if the people naturally met for
service at St. Hadrian's on that day as usual, but thence-
forward made it the starting-point for a procession to
St. Mary Major to keep there the festival of St. Mary's
Nativity. If it began thus, it would be found easy to
extend the association to the other three festivals. This
seems to have been done by Sergius (687–701).[b] The

[a] See, p. 24.   [b] *L. P.* i. 376.

observance of all the four feasts at Rome is not attested earlier than this.

Whence came these four feasts into the early Gelasian? Ultimately from the East;[a] and probably Jerusalem had a large share in their early history.[b] Not from or through Gallican channels, for the Gallican feast of our Lady[c] was principally that of January 18, which the *Missale Gothicum* calls *Assumptio S. Mariae matris domini nostri*, and the Bobbio Missal calls *Solemnitas S. Mariae*.[d] The link with the East runs probably through southern Italy; and in that case these feasts give further evidence that the Gelasian tradition is a suburban rite having close affinities with the south of Italy. In the Gregorian tradition the four feasts come in gradually. The Assumption is the earliest; then enters the Purification which seems to be the earliest in the East. The Nativity is adopted next, and last of all the Annunciation.[e]

Feb. 5. St. Agatha is a Sicilian not a Roman martyr. Her name was, therefore, not in the Early Roman Martyrology. But the interests of the Roman see in Sicily were considerable; and a transfer of her cult to Rome is therefore explained. The entry is common to Gelasian and Gregorian. Our earliest Gregorian authority **We** joins St. Agnes and St. Agatha together[f] (on Jan. 21?), giving them an epistle and three sapiential lessons. But perhaps this association, undated like all the feasts in this book, is only part of the policy which the compiler evidently pursued of grouping the lessons under headings. There is proper music provided both in the

[a] The name 'Hypapanti' shows this in the case of February 2.

[b] Duchesne, 272.

[c] The evidence goes back to Gregory of Tours (d. 595). Duchesne, 269.

[d] It adds also a Mass of the Roman type under the heading *Assumptio*.

[e] The Purification was observed by edict of Justinian at Constantinople in 542: and before the end of that century the Assumption was in use also. The other two are not attested earlier than the Council *in Trullo*, 692.

[f] Later Epistle-books do the same. See the Corbie Comes in Staerk, *MSS Latins*, p. 135, and the Comes of Verona, MS. lxxxii.

Gradual and the Antiphonal. The Introit *Gaudeamus* is
a non-biblical text; it was borrowed in some books for the
Assumption and for the Nativity. The Communion
takes its text from the Legend of the Saint. There is
no parallel to these texts anywhere else in the early
Gradual.[a] The music itself seems to belong to the
classical period.

The chief monument of the cult of St. Agatha was the
church in the Subura founded or restored about 470 by
Fl. Ricimer.[b] After a long association with Arianism,
whence came its later epithet *Gothorum*, it was re-dedi-
cated to Catholic worship by St. Gregory in 591 or 592.[c]
Possibly this is also the date of the adoption of this feast;
is it then also the date of the insertion of her name in the
Canon of the Mass?[d]

Feb. 14. Valentine. The entry is common to early
Gregorian and Gelasian. Some of the music provided for
it in the Gradual seems to be in its original position there,
and to have been borrowed thence for other days. A
church was built in honour of the saint at the Flaminian
gate (on the road to Terni) by Julius I (337–52), and
this must have brought the observance of his festival
within the orbit of Rome. It was repaired or rebuilt by
Honorius (625–8) and Theodore (642–9).[e]

[B.] Several feasts in February are found in the
Gelasian tradition which are not in the Gregorian.

Feb. 10. Soteris is a Roman Virgin and martyr commemorated on the *Via Appia*, who figures in the Early
Martyrology.[f] Other dates given there are February 6,
11. It is not clear why the liturgical observance in the

---

[a] Otherwise the use of non-biblical texts begins with later additions such as
the Dedication, Holy Cross Day, or the Vigil of the Assumption.
[b] Huelsen, 167.　　　　　　　　[c] *L. P.* i. 313.
[d] One early MS. of the Hieronymian Martyrology has a *nativitas* on July 25.
[e] *L. P.* i. 9, 206, 332, 334.
[f] See *Anal. Boll.* xlvi. 59, rather than Kirsch, 49, 137, 57.

Gelasian type was on the 10th; the 11th is attested by an
inscription of the year 401; so it must be held to be the
best attested of the three. Perhaps the liturgical observance was shifted to avoid a clash with SS. Parthenius
and Calocerus on the 11th; but, as these saints had no
early recognition in Kalendars, this is not a very attrac-
tive suggestion. The entry on the 6th may be only a
misreading of viii id. Feb. for iiii id. Feb.

In the 'Mixed' books there figures also on the 10th
a group of Roman martyrs, Zoticus Irenaeus and
Hyacinth.[a] On this date Zoticus is commemorated ten
miles out on the *Via Labicana*, with Amantius, in the
Old Roman Martyrology. Irenaeus has a more dubious
position among the entries there. Hyacinth is absent,
Zoticus and Amantius also appear on the 11th; so the
ambiguity already noticed in the case of Soteris reappears in their case. The four saints lay in different
parts of the cemetery, and were thus grouped together
in more or less numbers, and in varying order. Bede
records them all.

Feb. 14. In **V** the saints Vitalis and Felicula are
associated with Valentine both in the title and in the
Mass.[b] The later Mixed books add Zeno as well. Vitalis
is the saint of Spoleto, who has a prominent place on this
day in the Hieronymian Martyrology. Felicula has a
much more obscure place there; and the addition of her
name to or after the group, of which Vitalis is the leader,
may be due to the Gelasian influence. The Roman
virgin and martyr of that name belongs to June 5 or 13
(see below).

Zeno is added as a Roman saint at the end of the Bern
MS. of the Martyrology; and the saint is otherwise
attested. But the question arises why the entry was
made in 'Mixed' books; and whether that entry is the
source of the addition to the Martyrology.

[a] Kirsch, 137.   [b] Kirsch, 206 ff.

Feb. 17. Juliana belongs to Cumae and Pozzuoli,[a] and her festival forms part of the early Gelasian tradition **V**.

Feb. 22. Cathedra Petri. This is a Roman festival; and, as such, it is contrasted with the similar Gallican feast of January 18 (above p. 91). The entry runs back to the *Natale Petri de Cathedra* of the Philocalian Kalendar, but then for a time is unattested. Presumably a corresponding liturgical observance existed at some time in the Gelasian or Gregorian tradition, but there is no sign of it till the Frankish Mixed Books.[b] Some rival must have driven out the old Gallican feast of January 18, and presumably it is this Roman rival of February 22 that has done so. But in fact both the early Roman traditions, Gelasian and Gregorian alike, are without any such festival, so far as our existing authorities show. The Frankish Mixed Sacramentaries are responsible for its preservation, and so for its restoration to the later Roman rite. Its original disappearance may have been due to the unwillingness to place feasts on days in Lent when the solemn Stational Masses prevailed.

MARCH

is for this reason very barren. On the 7th the entry of Perpetua and Felicitas in the early Gelasian **V** preserved another festival, which was included in the Philocalian Kalendar, but does not figure in our early Gregorian authorities, perhaps because of the Lenten Stational Masses.

Two additions, however, are made as time goes on.

Mar. 12. St. Gregory does not appear early. The first signs of cult discernible are during the 8th century in the *Hadrianum*, the standard Gospel-lists, and the Gradual; and ecclesiologically under Leo III (795–816), the successor of Hadrian.[c]

---

[a] Lanzoni, 208.

[b] The Reichenau Palimpsest has it between Quinquagesima and Quadragesima (ed. Dold, p. 15).   [c] *L. P.* ii. 10, 18.

Mar. 25. The Annunciation of the B.V.M., like the other great feasts of the B.V. Mary, is in **V**; but it is very slow to make its way into the Gregorian tradition. It is not in the early Gospel-books but appears in the *Hadrianum.* The early Gradual and Antiphonal alike show that it had to borrow its music from earlier sources.[a]

APRIL

is also a barren mouth. The Gelasian **V** gives only one feast, Euphemia; and that is one not contained in the Gregorian list. The ancient Gregorian entries are three.

		11. Leo.
	13. Euphemia.	
22. Tiburtius Valerian and Maximus.		
		23. George.
25. Litania maior.		
28. Vitalis.		

[A.] Apr. 14. The cult of Tiburtius is recognized in the Leonine Sacramentary, for his name is mentioned in a Preface[b] included in Section VIII, the collection of Saints-day Masses in April, in the midst of which the MS., as we now have it, begins. The saint and his companions, Valerius and Maximus, were famous in Rome, from their connexion with St. Cecilia, and from their own underground church in the catacomb of Praetextatus. There is a proper Introit for this day.

Apr. 25. The *Litania maior* is a Roman institution unknown to the early Gelasian tradition. On April 25 the pagan procession of the *Robigalia* was superseded by a corresponding Christian procession. The earliest evidence for a Litany of this kind comes from the time of St. Gregory.[c] His Register contains a formula of announce-

---

[a] See above, p. 92.

[b] Ed. Feltoe, p. 1. This preface was later used with additions for St. Stephen. See *Gregorian Sacr.* (ed. Wilson), p. 232.

[c] *M.G.H., Greg. Registr.* i. 102; but the date is uncertain (see Grisar, 88), and the identification of Gregory's procession with that of April 25 is also insecure.

ment of a Litania maior in the year 598. Two Gospels are provided for the day in the earliest Capitularies; the procession and the Mass are found in the *Hadrianum*, and proper music in the Gradual. The usage passed from the Gregorian tradition into the Mixed Sacramentaries; but found itself in opposition to the Gallican custom of holding three Litanies on the three days preceding Ascension Day, which had been in general use since the Council of Orleans prescribed it in 511.[a] Ultimately the Gallican custom prevailed over the Roman, the 'Rogationes' over the 'Litania maior'. The term 'maior' marks the contrast not between the procession in April and those preceding Ascension; for it was in use in St. Gregory's time; but the contrast between the procession in April and the usual processions leading up to the Stational Mass, or appointed for other occasions. In the time of Leo III (795–816) the notice of the great procession was given at the St. George's Day service.[b]

Apr. 28. Vitalis. The title-church *Vestinae*, situated *in Vico Longo*, was founded by a matron called Vestina, and was dedicated by Innocent I (401–17).[c] The *Liber Pontificalis* gives a specially full account of the foundation. Originally the dedication was to the famous Milanese SS. Gervasius and Protasius, whose reputation spread widely after St. Ambrose had found their relics in 386. The signatures to the Roman Council of 595 show, that by the end of the 6th century the dedication to St. Vitalis, as the reputed father of the Milanese martyrs, had come into use; and the new dedication tended to oust both the earlier names of the church.[d] This St. Vitalis is probably the same person as the companion of Agricola,[e] venerated specially at Bologna. The invention of the bodies of these two saints took place at Milan in the

---

[a] Bruns, *Canones*, ii. 165.   [b] *L. P.* ii. 35, 40.   [c] *L. P.* i. 220.
[d] Kirsch, *Die Römischen Titelkirchen*, pp. 68–70; *Analecta Bollandiana*, xlvi. 55 ff.   [e] Kirsch, 143.

G 2

presence of St. Ambrose in 393; the date of their festival, however, there is November 27.[a] The Roman feast is found in the early Gregorian Capitularies; it has proper music in the Gradual. It may be supposed that it is the Dedication Festival of the church at Rome.

[B.] Apr. 13. A notable entry in the Gelasian book is that of St. Euphemia on April 13; it is contrasted with the entry in the *Leonianum*, Sections XXIV, XXV, on September 16.[b] The feast reappears on that date in the Gregorian. On both dates it is the martyr of Chalcedon who is in question. Out of Rome her festival was usually kept on April 13; perhaps the rival date in September was the festival of the church dedicated to St. Euphemia on the Viminal near St. Pudentiana, which was restored by Sergius I (687–701).[c]

[C.] Apr. 23. At a later stage St. George is added on April 23, both in the Gregorian and in the Mixed Sacramentaries; and the Masses provided vary. The date of the introduction of this cult is obscure. If the name 'Gregory martyr' in the *Leonianum* is a miswriting for 'George', the date is carried back into the 6th century. The position of the Mass there in April (VIII, § XXIII) favours this view. But there may be some obscure Gregory who is intended, like the Gregory who is associated with St. Chrysogonus on his day (Nov. 24, § XXXVIII). The Gregorian Mass of St. George differs wholly from the Leonine Mass in question, and is in no respect Leonine; so no direct connexion is traceable. The Gregorian lists show that St. George's Day is not an early feature of that tradition (p. 60); but the Gradual seems to show that there was some music special to the day.

Clearer evidence is found in the selection of St. George's Church to be the place of Station on the first

[a] Delehaye, 374.   [b] Also there in the Martyrology of Carthage.
[c] *L. P.* i. 375, 380. See below, p. 130.

Thursday in Lent, after Gregory II (715–31) had made the Thursdays liturgical days. This choice did not carry with it a place in the Kalendar, but it is evidence of special cult. Perhaps the fixing of this Station is to be ascribed not to Gregory but to his next-but-one successor Zacharias (741–52); for he enriched the existing diaconal church of St. George in Velabro (*ad velum aureum*) with the head of St. George, which he found in his palace. The earlier history of the church is not clear;[a] but its rise into prominence seems to go by natural stages, from being diaconal to being stational, and then to acquiring a place in the Kalendar about the time of the *Hadrianum*.

Apr. 11. Leo is given on this date in the Mixed Sacramentaries. The entry is discussed below at June 28 (p. 115).

MAY

1. Philip and James.

3. Alexander Eventius and Theodulus; Juvenal; Invention of H. Cross.
6. St. John Port-Latin.
10. Gordian. Epimachus.

12. Nereus and Achilles; Pancras.

13. Dedication of St. Mary ad martyres.
19. Pudentiana.
25. Urban.

[A.] May 1. SS. Philip and James. This day is common to both Gelasian and Gregorian, and it has proper music in the Gradual and Antiphonal. It is the dedication Festival of the Church of the Apostles or *Basilica Julia*, built originally by Julius (337–52), rebuilt under Pelagius I (555–60) and John III his successor. It was dedicated at the rebuilding, or earlier, to SS. Philip and James, but it was usually called *Basilica Apostolorum*, and

---

[a] *L. P.* i. 434, 439. See also a dubious piece of evidence added to the life of Leo II (682–3); ibid. 360, 362.

appears as such in the list of Stations on a number of occasions, including the Ember seasons.

May 12. SS. Nereus and Achilles became the patrons of the *titulus Fasciolae*, and they are found in the Old Roman Martyrology with a reference to their shrines in their own cemetery, which formed part of the catacomb of Domitilla on the *Via Ardeatina*.[a]

St. Pancras appears with them in the Martyrology; his cemeterial church two miles out on the *Via Aurelia* was founded or rebuilt by Symmachus (498–514)[b] and restored by Honorius I (625–38).[c]

In the early Gregorian authorities the two commemorations are kept separate, for the capitularies provide a Gospel for each. But the Gelasian tradition joins them in one Mass—naturally enough if it represents the provincial and not the urban point of view. In the *Hadrianum* Nereus and Achilles are omitted, and there is only the Mass of St. Pancras. There are various pieces of evidence, that, for a time, the church in Rome lost its status. It dropped out of the list of *tituli*, and became merely a deaconry (see above p. 13). It also ceased to be the Stational Church of XL[6]ii, and St. Praxedis for a time took its place (above p. 20). This situation is all of a piece with the disappearance of the festival in **H** and in **P**, and equally in the early Gradual (Pam).

In the later Gregorian books as in the Mixed Sacramentaries the three saints are fused in one Commemoration. The Gradual then contains a proper introit *Ecce oculi*, which had been given indifferently to either of the two separately, and serves for them when combined. As it is phrased in the plural, presumably it belonged in its origin to SS. Nereus and Achilles.

[a] Kirsch, 57. The Bern MS. wrongly gives the cemetery of Praetextatus. In their church Gregory delivered his Homily, No. xxviii in Evang.

[b] *L. P.* i. 46, 262, 266.

[c] Huelsen, 409.

[B.] Turning now to the entries which are not common to Gelasian and Gregorian we note as follows.

May 3. SS. Alexander Eventius and Theodulus appear in the Gregorian, not in the Gelasian tradition. This group of martyrs figured in the Old Roman Martyrology,[a] as commemorated in the catacomb of Alexander, seven miles away on the *Via Nomentana*. Alexander's name then held the second place in order; but later it was put first, probably because he was identified with the early Pope Alexander I. Their sepulchral church was discovered in 1855; the bodies had been translated to St. Sabina's.[b]

The Gelasian compilers found Juvenal, the first bishop of Narni,[c] more interesting than the trio of Roman martyrs. The Mixed Sacramentaries found room for both; and later books combined them in one commemoration.

Further, on this date the Gelasian has the Invention of the Cross. A Mass for this feast is found in Gallican books, after Low Sunday in the *Missale Gothicum*, and before Ascension in the Bobbio Missal;[d] but these two are different one from another; both of them, equally in structure and style, are entirely unlike the Gelasian Mass. It is unlikely, therefore, that the feast came to the Gelasian from Gaul. It is more likely that it came to both independently from the East; and that the channel in the case of the Gelasian was southern Italy. This supposition is confirmed by the fact that the Gelasian has also the Exaltation of the Cross on September 14; there is no sign of this in the early Gallican books. It must have come from the East, probably after 628 when Heraclius recovered the Cross from the Persians.

[a] Kirsch, 146.   [b] Marucchi, 188; *L. P.* i. xci.

[c] He was twice mentioned by St. Gregory as a famous martyr (*Hom. in Ev.* xxxviii. 9; and *Dial.* iv. 12).

[d] *Missale Gothicum* (*H. B. S.*) i. 92; and *Bobbio Missal* (*H. B. S.*), Text, p. 86.

The Invention did not find its way into the *Hadrianum*, but it is in **P**, the Paduan MS. of the Gregorian Sacramentary. It is found in some of the early Graduals. Most of the music there is borrowed and serves for the two feasts of Holy Cross jointly, but there are two alternative Communions found, which are proper; and occasionally also there is a proper Offertory. Two of these three pieces are non-biblical texts.

In the Antiphonal there is a considerable amount of proper music, some applicable to either festival, some belonging only to the Invention, but it is nearly all of late date.

All points to the late date of the festival in Roman-Gregorian use.

May 6. St. John *ante Portam Latinam*. There is no evidence of this feast that is earlier than **P** and **H**. The church that had of old been built at the Latin Gate to commemorate the escape of St. John the Evangelist from the boiling oil was rebuilt by Hadrian (772–95),[a] and the entry is probably due to this event. But there seems to have been a corresponding 'Gelasian' feast of the Evangelist, to judge by the marginal entry 'Natl. S. Johannis Evang.' in the Barberini Gospel-capitulary (p. 75), and the fact that the Capuan Gospel-list (p. 48[c]) provides for a second festival of St. John besides the 'Assumptio' on December 27.

May 10. Gordian. This entry is usual in early Gregorian Capitularies and Graduals, and it corresponds with the notice in the early Roman Martyrology.[b] It is not found in the early Gelasian. In **H** Epimachus is joined with Gordian in a Mass which differs markedly from that in the Mixed books. Epimachus is also a Roman martyr, mentioned in the early Martyrology, but separately from Gordian. The two saints lay apart, but close to one another, on the *Via Latina*. They came to have a church

[a] *L. P.* i. 508, 521.   [b] Kirsch, 54.

in common, which was rebuilt by Hadrian (772–95).[a] The liturgical association of the two probably dates from that event.

May 13. *Dedicatio ecclesiae S. Mariae ad martyres.*

On this day in 609 (?) Boniface IV set apart the temple of the Pantheon to serve as a Christian church.[b] It became a Stational Church, where the service was held on the Octave of Christmas and the Friday in Easter week.

Proper music was provided for the day. It is therefore in origin slightly later than the Gregorian revision of the chant, but written before the decay of the musical art set in. It is noticeable, however, that the Gradual is set to a non-biblical text.

The entry is not in **We,** but is in **R.** This fact seems to suggest that the date did not find a permanent place in the Kalendar till after the time of Gregory II; for his successor Gregory III (731–41) restored the church;[c] and probably it was this restoration that brought the festival into general use. But it soon went out again in favour of the different dedication days of the various churches.

The question of its connexion with All Saints' Day will be discussed below.

May 19. Pudentiana. This is the saint who came into being as patroness of the *titulus Pudentis.* Naturally, therefore, such an entry in the Kalendar is slow to make its appearance. In the early Capitularies the name is given but no Gospel. The numbering of the Gospels in the Capitulary of Faron [d] takes no account of it. Though the Capitularies include it, the *Hadrianum* does not, nor the early Mixed Sacramentaries. The Graduals agree generally with the Capitularies; but it is noticeable that the music is borrowed from St. Lucy. It is evident that the festival obtained recognition only with difficulty. Possibly

[a] *L. P.* i. 509, 521. [b] *L. P.* i. 317. [c] *L. P.* i. 419.
[d] Bodleian Library, MS. Douce 176.

the critical objection was to some extent felt, that the saint had a fictitious origin, being merely hypostatized from the *titulus*.

May 25. Urban is not found in the early Gregorian or Gelasian. The feast first appears in the Carolingian Capitularies, as commemorated on the *Via Appia*, and it is also in the *Hadrianum*; subsequently it came into the Mixed Sacramentaries, but there the Mass is different.

The person intended is, no doubt, Urban I,[a] who was buried according to the *Liber Pontificalis* in the cemetery of Praetextatus on the *Via Appia*. But there has been some confusion with another Bishop Urban, whose day is May 19. This confusion shows itself both in the later form of the Martyrology and in the *Liber Pontificalis*. The late appearance of the feast is noteworthy. The fact is that the Deposition of Pope Urban (d. 230) was not recorded in the Philocalian list, nor was the entry in the early Martyrology; the date (25th) comes from his *Passio*. Some revival of interest must have brought in the feast by the end of the 8th century. It cannot have been the translation of the relics to St. Cecilia's church, for that did not take place till Pope Paschal's time, 821.[b]

JUNE

1. Nicomede.

2. Peter and Marcellinus.

9. Primus and Felician.
12. Basilides; Nabor and Nazarius; Cyrinus.
14. Felicula.
15. Vitus.

18. Mark and Marcellian.
19. Gervasius and Protasius.
23. Vigil of St. John Baptist.
24. John Baptist.
26. John and Paul.
28. Vigil.   Transl. of Leo (668).
29. Peter and Paul.
30. Paul.

[a] Kirsch, 19, 110–12; *L. P.* i. 143.   [b] *L. P.* ii. 56.

[A.] The last six of the early entries go back to the *Leonianum*, and the first three also are common to the Gregorian and Gelasian traditions.

June 2. SS. Peter and Marcellinus. This is the order of the names in the early liturgical authorities; but the inverse order is that of the Old Martyrology and of most of the later Service-books. The martyrs were commemorated four miles out on the *Via Labicana* in their cemetery, also called *Inter duas lauros*. Damasus wrote their epitaph[a] after hearing, as a boy, the account of their death from the executioner himself. The cult goes back to early days. They became the patrons of the old *titulus Nicomedis* (*Matthaei*), which was the Station-church on XL²vii, and some proper music is provided in the Gradual.

June 18. SS. Mark and Marcellian. This entry is in early Service-books; the commemoration was noted in the early Martyrology as being held in the cemetery of Balbina on the *Via Nomentana* in the church erected over their tombs.[b] John VII (705–7) busied himself with this site;[c] and if the entry of the festival here is not of earlier date, it was probably added then. The bodies of the saints were translated into the church of SS. Cosmas and Damian probably in the 9th century, and they were found there in the 16th.[d]

June 19. SS. Gervasius and Protasius. Their relation to the *titulus Vestinae* has already been described under Vitalis (April 28). In the Carolingian Capitularies the direction is given here *ad S. Vitalem*, to show that the service was held there on this day.

The feast is common to early Gelasian and Gregorian; but a vigil is found only in the Gelasian tradition.

June 23–30. At this point the *Leonianum* first comes

---

[a] Ihm, No. 29, p. 34.
[c] *L. P.* i. 385–6.

[b] Kirsch, 155.
[d] Marucchi, *Basiliques*, 859.

in as direct evidence of the festival-list. It contains John the Baptist, John and Paul, Peter and Paul.

June 23. The vigil is provided for St. John Baptist, but not for the others. In **V** there is a vigil for SS. John and Paul which survives into some Mixed Sacramentaries. It is not easy to say why these two vigils should exist in this month according to the Gelasian tradition.

June 26. SS. John and Paul are the patrons of the *titulus Pammachii* or *Byzantis* on the Caelian. The foundation of Pammachius[a] must be dated in the early years of the 5th century before his death in 410. Perhaps the title *Byzantis* refers to an earlier foundation on the same spot; for the remains of a house of the 3rd century underlie the church. It is not easy to say when the dedication to SS. John and Paul took place. The Legend of the Saints, which belongs to the 6th century, is arbitrarily built up on a few names. Its theory that they were martyrs under Julian is one not easily reconcilable with the early names of the church—*Byzantis* and *Pammachius*. The builder's name was, as a rule, the first name given, and the dedication in the name of a saint or saints came later. This dedication is not mentioned (independently of the Legend) till early in the 6th century.[b]

These saints have a shadowy existence; their place in the Roman Martyrology is a dubious one, and the entry is probably not a genuine entry of Roman martyrs, but one borrowed from liturgical or ecclesiological sources. The excavations under the church, while they reveal the primitive church erected out of a Roman house, discredit rather than corroborate the legend of John and Paul.

The suggestion has been made that the dedication was originally to the Apostles John and Paul,[c] just as the Basilica Julia was dedicated to SS. Philip and James

---

[a] Kirsch, 159; and Kirsch, *Titelk.* 26 ff.
[b] On a tombstone of 535. Ibid. 28.   [c] Delehaye, *Culte des Martyrs*, 341.

(*c.* 350). But two *a priori* objections at once arise; first that any such association of St. Paul is unlikely in Rome, and second that if the patrons were apostles it is not likely that obscure martyrs would be substituted for them. On the other hand, the suggestion meets the archaeological difficulty, and accounts for the unusual interest, that in the early days was taken by the Roman Church, as is evidenced by the fact that the early Gelasian provides a vigil for the feast, and that there is proper music both in the Gradual and the Antiphonal.

The Leonine Masses of the day include one (No. 5) which (alone)[a] mentions the two saints. The two points which are brought out are these; in the Collect, that the saints became brothers in faith and in martyrdom; in the Preface, that it is remarkable to find relics in the heart of the city as well as in the suburban cemeteries.[b] This is noteworthy, but it probably does not carry us behind the rise of the Legend in the 6th century.

The second point made might, indeed, be inserted as a reply to an obvious criticism to which the Legend was open, viz. that no martyr of the time of Julian would be buried within the walls.

Whatever be thought of the suggestion, the early incorporation of the festival into the Kalendar is clear.

June 29. SS. Peter and Paul. The observance of a joint feast of these Apostles does not rest upon the history of their deaths. They were martyred in two different spots outside Rome, and presumably at different times. They were early associated in men's minds as joint founders of the Roman Church; and when the cult of the martyrs began in the 3rd century, it was natural to give them a joint festival. The Philocalian Kalendar gives at June 29 their 'depositions' thus: *Petri ad Catacumbas et*

[a] The first three of the eight Masses are included earlier in the block of Saints-days in April, § viii, 39–41.

[b] This is the Mass given in **V** and **H**. They lack a Preface but provide for a postcommunion which is lacking in **L**.

Pauli Ostense, and adds the consular date of the year 258. These Apostles are the only martyrs of the Roman Church previous to the 3rd century that are there entered.[a] The addition of a date is unusual;[b] it probably records the institution of the joint festival, but the occasion of that institution remains obscure. It can hardly have been unconnected with the persecution of Valerian.[c] The usual explanation is that at that date the bodies of St. Peter and St. Paul were translated temporarily to the church of St. Sebastian on the Appian Way. The recent investigations made on the spot have shown good proof of the veneration of the two Apostles there in the 3rd century and later; but they do not in any way help to account for it.[d] A joint sojourn of the Saints *ad catacumbas* is noted in some of the forms which the entry takes in the early Martyrology, *Romae Petri et Pauli: Petri in Vaticano, Pauli Via Ostiensi, utrumque in Catacumbas.* This is more correct than the earlier notice, at least so far as St. Peter's resting in the Vatican is concerned, and it seems to distinguish a joint later burial from the original and separate burials.

We come to the liturgical observance as depicted in the *Leonianum.* There are twenty-eight Masses provided. The heading is *In N. Apostolorum Petri et Pauli* to the first; then *Item alia* for Nos. ii–xxv. At xxvi we read *Item ad S. Paulum,* followed by *Item alia* for the two remaining. There is no direction *Ad Catacumbas,* nor anything that suggests a sojourn of the bodies there in St. Sebastian's Church. It is archaeology rather than liturgy that comes to the support of the martyrology in this matter.

[a] Callistus (Oct. 14, 222) otherwise is the earliest entry.
[b] Two other instances—May 19 and September 22—have 304.
[c] See the discussion in Delehaye, *Culte des Martyrs,* 302–8; and the examination of the text in Kirsch, *Rivista di Archeol. Christ.* (1925), pp. 56 ff.
[d] On St. Sebastian see Chéramy, *Saint-Sébastien* (Paris, 1925); *Röm. Quartalschrift,* xxxv; *J. T. S.* (1926), xxviii. 30–9, 262.

The Sacramentary distinguishes one Mass, or perhaps three Masses, as meant to be said at St. Paul's: this seems to imply that the earlier ones are for St. Peter's. No date of the month is given in this section; elsewhere dates are usually (though not always) prefixed. It is indubitable that June 29 is the date intended at the heading; but it is not so certain to assume that the Mass *Ad S. Paulum* is meant for the day following, as is usual in later books. It is known from a hymn, which is probably a genuine composition of St. Ambrose, that the feast was kept in the three places in his day.[a] But there is no reference here to St. Sebastian's as a place where the festival was to be kept.

It is true of all the Masses provided in the *Leonianum*, which are at all distinctive,[b] that the service was for both Apostles.[c] Some of the Masses seem to imply the observance of the octave. There is no Mass either for St. Peter or for St. Paul separately; they are throughout regarded as the joint founders of the see of Rome.

The position is altered in the early Gregorian. Our most ancient authority **We** has a vigil of St. Peter and a feast of St. Peter, followed by a vigil of St. Paul and a feast of St. Paul, with Epistles corresponding. Similarly some early capitularies. The bulk of them, however, have a vigil and a feast of SS. Peter and Paul, and on the 30th the heading *ad S. Paulum* with another Gospel concerning St. Peter (Matt. xix. 27–9). Later, again, the *Hadrianum* has a vigil and *Natale* of St. Peter followed by a *Natale* of St. Paul; but all the contents apply to both apostles, except a Collect provided for Vespers of St. Peter's Day and the Mass Collect of St. Paul.

[a] 'Trinis celebratur viis Festum sanctorum martyrum.' From the hymn, 'Apostolorum passio', *Anal. Hymn.* L. 18.

[b] Half the Masses make no allusion to SS. Peter and Paul, but only to Apostles: No. 21 speaks of *omnium apostolorum*, No. 15 of martyrdom only.

[c] No. 26 has a specially long Preface balancing the one with the other.

The early Gradual has the same three occasions, but the musical texts correspond to the titles. They refer to St. Peter on the two former days, and to St. Paul on the third. This arrangement is perhaps due to St. Gregory if his biographer Paul the Deacon, writing *c.* 875, is to be trusted.[a]

Coming back to the Gelasian **V**, we find a vigil of SS. Peter and Paul on the 28th; a *Natale S. Petri proprie*, a *Natale* of SS. Peter and Paul, a *Natale S. Pauli proprie* on the 30th, followed by a series of *Orationes ad Vesperum*, referring to both; then, undated, a vigil and a *Natale Omnium Apostolorum*, besides the octave of SS. Peter and Paul. This provision seems to be a combination of the earlier and the later methods of keeping the days, with a 'Common of Apostles' subjoined. The earlier method draws upon the same store as the *Leonianum* very largely; the set of Vesper Collects and the Common of Apostles does the same. The *proprie* Masses, when they do the same, modify the language to fit the new purpose.

The books of later date represent different stages and combinations.

Such variety at this point is unexpected and puzzling. Perhaps it represents no more than a difference of use at St. Peter's from the general use, the former tending to isolate St. Peter at the expense of St. Paul.

[B.] June 1. St. Nicomede. This is the first of the additions to be considered. It is of late Gregorian origin. It does not appear even in the Carolingian standard Capitulary; but it is entered in **P, H** as *Dedicatio basilice S. Nicomedis*. The basilica in question is probably not the cemeterial church restored by Boniface V (619–25),[b] but another urban church rebuilt by Hadrian. The dedication festival is apparently earlier than Hadrian's

---

[a] Hic fecit ut super corpus beati Petri et Pauli apostolorum missae celebrentur. *P. L.* LXXV. Cp. Micrologus in *P. L.* CLI, 1009.

[b] *L. P.* i. 321, 322, 511.

time, for it is in **P**, which represents an earlier stage of Gregorian than **H**.

June 9. SS. Primus and Felician. They are entered in the early Martyrology [a] as being commemorated on the *Via Nomentana* fifteen miles out *ad arcas*, that is at Nomentum itself. The distance was too great a one to travel from Rome for a service. Probably for this reason the bodies were translated by Theodore (642–9) to the church of St. Stephen on the Caelian, which he was restoring.[b] This translation has the credit of being the first instance of the policy of bringing the saints' bodies from the cemeteries situated outside Rome into the churches within the walls. It probably originated the observance of this day in the papal Kalendar. For, though the entry is not found in **H** or **P**, it is in the early Gospel-books;[c] and in some of them, especially in the Martina group, the direction is given *in basilica S. Stephani.*

June 12. St. Basilides is entered in the early Martyrology on June 10, as being commemorated fourteen miles out along the *Via Aurelia*; on June 12 the same entry occurs but the number of miles is five.[d] The martyr was in due course provided with a *Passio*, and found a place in one of our early Gregorian Capitularies (**Wg**), misplaced on the 12th, and in **Jon** undated; in **R** there was no such entry; and where it occurs there is only the heading, and a blank filled by no Gospel.

This, however, shows that in some quarters the entry was included in the Gregorian Kalendar by the beginning of the 8th century, though it is absent from Hadrian. The introit *Gloria et honore* seems to belong properly to

---

[a] Kirsch, 59.
[b] *L. P.* i. 332.
[c] Not infrequently on the 8th. **Wg** has it out of place.
[d] Kirsch, 60 ff. The church of St. Basilides is not otherwise attested till the restoration by Leo III (795–816). See *L. P.* ii. 29, 47.

this day; and if so, the date might safely be put back a century earlier.

June 12. Cyrinus, Nabor and Nazarius. This is the early Gelasian entry in **V** on the 12th. Cyrinus is probably the bishop of Siscia, while the others are the famous Milanese pair.[a] A church had been built in their honour at Rome as early as the beginning of the 5th century. It stood four or five miles out on the *Via Aurelia*. The reason for the association of Cyrinus with this day is not clear. His body is said to have been translated to Rome in the 4th century when Pannonia was overrun, and to have been buried in the basilica of the Apostles on the *Via Appia*. The crypt containing an inscription in his honour, dating from the early 5th century,[b] has recently come to light during the excavations *ad catacumbas*.[c]

It seems clear, however, that the cult of Basilides has been fused with the other because of the local proximity. Possibly the original commemoration of Basilides was held fifteen miles out on the 10th; but it was found better to unite it with the festival held ten miles nearer the city on the 12th. The fusion is found in the Mixed Sacramentaries, and occasionally in one form of the Standard Gospel-capitulary.

June 5, 13, 14. Felicula the Roman martyr buried seven miles out on the *Via Ardeatina* is confidently mentioned in the Old Roman Martyrology[d] on June 5, and more dubiously on the 13th. The Standard Gospel-list contained her name on the 14th; but it disappeared again quickly.

June 15. St. Vitus of Lucania is one of the south Italian saints which the Gelasian tradition favoured.[e] The entry is an early one in the Martyrology. The later legend provided for him is fantastic; from it was taken

---

[a] Kirsch, 62 & ff.   [b] Ihm, Damasus Epigr. 76 a.
[c] Chéramy, *Saint-Sébastien*, &c., *ut sup.* p. 88.   [d] Kirsch, 154.
[e] See **V** and p. 41; Delehaye, 352.

the later custom of associating Modestus, his tutor, and Crescentia, his nurse, with him on this day.

This entry is found in some Gospel-capitularies on this day; perhaps this is due to the deaconry. But in others St. Vitus is added on June 4.

June 28. Translation of Leo. This took place on that day under Sergius in 688.[a] The entry is not found, therefore, in the earlier documents. The first liturgical evidence of this comes from the group of 'Martina' Capitularies, and the historical evidence from the inscription which Sergius put up. In fact there is some confusion prevailing. The *Liber Pontificalis*[b] says that Leo was buried at St. Peter's on April 11. The Old Roman Martyrology rightly gives the original *Depositio* on November 10, for this date agrees with the accession of Hilary, his successor, on the 17th.[c] One, however, of the early texts gives, probably as a Gallican addition, *Romae Leonis papae* at April 11. This is the date of the '*Natale*' in the Mixed Mass-books; and it must be a Gallican or Gelasian insertion there, for the *Natale* in **H** (not in **P**) stands at June 28, with quite a different Mass—that is on the day which the group of Capitularies assigns to a 'Translation'. Liturgical usage has thus varied between these two dates; and the date in November, so well attested in the Martyrologies, is strangely ignored in the Service-books. Leo's election had taken place on September 29, so the term 'Natale' cannot at either date be referred to his *dies natalis* as Pope. The mistaken tradition that his deposition took place on April 11 is not only found in the *Liber Pontificalis*, but implied in the inscription of Sergius. This tradition has finally prevailed.[d]

[a] *L. P.* i. 375, 379.   [b] *L. P.* i. 239, 241; Kirsch, 117.
[c] *Acta SS.*, at April 11.
[d] The confusion has caused the festival of June 28 to be referred to Leo II (d. 683): but the *Liber Pontificalis* says expressly that he held an ordination on June 27 and was buried on July 3. Besides it is hardly likely that the *Hadrianum* would have commemorated him and not Leo I.

JULY

July is another barren month. The Octave of the Apostles is not found in the Leonine, though the existence there of twenty-eight Masses would amply provide for an octave; and the phrases *saepius iterata solemnitas* in No. 20 and *solemnitatis apostolicae multiplicatio* in No. 28 suggest that such an observance was contemplated. Apart from this there are three feasts which may go back to the groundwork.

2. Processus and Martinian.

6. Octave of the Apostles.
10. Septem Fratres.
21. Praxedis.

11. Benedict.

23. Apollinaris.
25. James the Apostle.
29. Felix; Simplicius Faustinus and Beatrice.

30. Abdon and Sennen.

[A.] July 10. Septem Fratres. The first of these feasts is found in the Leonine, Section XVII. It is not in the early Gelasian; and the Mass found in the **H** and the Mixed Sacramentaries is independent of the Leonine Masses of the day, though it contains some material used elsewhere in the *Leonianum*.

July 21. Praxedis. The feast of St. Praxedis is doubtless due to the 'title' of that name, *titulus Praxedis*. On that ground it has been given a position in the above list; but it must be admitted that its claims to that position are not very secure. For though it is found in most of the early Gospel-books[a] where the list is a complete one, it is not in the early Sacramentaries nor in the early Martyrology.

July 30. Abdon and Sennen. These saints were buried *via Portuensi, in cimiterio Pontiani ad ursum pileatum*, as is known from the Early Martyrology, and the Philocalian Kalendar.

[a] It is misplaced in **Wg**.

It may further be noted that each of the first two of these three feasts seems to have music of its own. The third has not, and indeed the music allotted to it varies in the different early authorities. But its liturgical observance seems sure; for it is found in **P**, marked *Via Portuense*, and in **H**; earlier evidence is afforded by the earliest Gospel-books, and in them two Gospels are assigned to it.

July 10. The first of these entries requires a little more explanation before we pass on to the additional entries. Septem Fratres is the name of a group of Roman martyrs who suffered various deaths and were buried in various places, but were all commemorated on the one day. The list given in the Philocalian Kalendar reappears in the *Leonianum*, Section XVII. Januarius lay *ad Aquilonem*[a] in the catacomb of Praetextatus on the *Via Appia*; Felix and Philip lay in the catacomb of Priscilla on the *Via Salaria Nova*; Vitalis, Martial and Alexander on the same road in the cemetery of the *Jordani*, at a place called from the last of the group *ad Alexandrum*; Silanus close by in the cemetery of Maximus, which was called also *ad Felicitatem*, because the Roman matron commemorated on November 23 was buried there. These seven came to be regarded as brothers, and as the sons of Felicitas. One of the Leonine Masses for the Seven refers to the former point;[b] and those for Felicitas imply her having seven martyred sons.[c] The earlier Capitularies provide Gospels for three Masses, *Prima missa ad Aquilonem; Secunda ad S. Alexandrum; ubi supra ad S. Felicitatem.*[d] Some also add to the heading the note *Appia, Salaria.* But it is not clear how far the connexion

[a] This title is found in a description of this area given in the Salzburg Itinerary. De Rossi, *Roma Sotteranea*, i. 180.

[b] The third; it is the only one of the seven Masses provided that has special reference to the day.

[c] Leonine, § XXXVII.

[d] The reference to the catacomb of Priscilla has dropped out. TA has *Via Appia ad S. Januarium: item Via Salaria prima missa ad Aquilonem, secunda ad S. Alexandrum.* Cp. Zf.

between the festival of the Seven and the festival of St. Felicitas is a genuine one. A rival identification brought her into connexion with another group of Seven —the Machabees commemorated on August 1; but this seems to be of later date. The Gospel-capitularies[a] which transported her Gospel from November 23 to August 1 are not of early date.

Besides in early (418–22) days two of the groups that go to make up the Seven had inscriptions of their own, Felix and Philip from Damasus;[b] and Vitalis Martial and Alexander from Vigilius (536–55); and in them there is no genuine mention of Felicitas.

[B.] July 28, 29. SS. Felix, Simplicius, Faustinus, and Beatrice.

In considering the additions to this list for July it may be well to begin with one which has a local connexion with the festival of Abdon and Sennen, and preceded it on the 29th. Three miles out on that same *Via Portuensis* was a church of St. Felix, apparently built by Pope Julius († 352).[c] Much confusion existed between him and the anti-pope Felix (II), who seems to have lived on the *Via Portuensis*, but to have been buried on the *Via Aurelia*, and commemorated on December 22.[d] But the entries in the Martyrologies are puzzling. There is a Felix entered at July 29 but 'in Africa'.

Three miles farther along the *Via Portuensis* were buried three Roman martyrs, SS. Simplicius, Faustinus, and Beatrice, 'super Philippi, miliario VI, in cimiterio eorundem' as the early Martyrology seems to have recorded.[e] The early Gelasian took no account of St. Felix, but only of the trio. The Mixed Sacramentaries had a Mass for each. The two commemorations evidently

[a] Lb &c.; Pa &c.

[b] Ed. Ihm, Nos. 47, 89: cp. ibid., No. 41, the spurious inscription about Felicitas. Delehaye, 313.

[c] *L. P.* i. cxxiii–v, 9, 71, 158, 205, 206, 211.

[d] Kirsch, 73, 185–8.　　　　　[e] Kirsch, 73, 26.

were combined for convenience sake. The combination brought about different results.

The Gospel-books provided a Gospel of many martyrs, mentioning all four saints. **H** also mentions all four in the heading, but the Mass in fact concerns only St. Felix. There is ambiguity also as to the date. The Gospel-books and **H** vary between the 28th and the 29th. The early Gelasian says for the trio v *Kal. seu potius* iv *Kal. Aug.* The Mixed Sacramentaries put the trio on the 28th and St. Felix on the 29th.

It is, however, to be noted that Leo II (681–3) built a church of St. Paul near St. Bibiana in Rome[a] to which he translated the bodies of SS. Simplicius Faustinus and Beatrice on February 22. The reason for the combination then disappeared; the presumption therefore is that it was made before this translation took place. St. Gregory in his 13th Gospel-homily, delivered on this feast,[b] referred only to St. Felix. It would seem, therefore, that the combination began in the first half of the 7th century. The connexion when once made was carried on even after the bodies had been moved into a new and more accessible position within the walls of the city.

The music-books throw some light upon the matter. The Introit *Sacerdotes eius* seems to belong originally to St. Felix, and to have been borrowed thence for Pope Stephen. The Mass is provided as for a pope, no doubt because he was thought to be the anti-pope Felix, or possibly Felix I. It continued to be used, though not always in identically the same form, after the combination with the trio, even when the name of Felix dropped out of the title and only the trio remained.

July 2. On this day the Gospel-books have Processus and Martinian: a corresponding Mass appears in **H**, which was taken over bodily by the Mixed Books. The church, which was two miles out on the *Via Aurelia*, had long

[a] *L. P.* i. 361. Huelsen, 415.   [b] *P. L.* LXXVI. 1123.

been the centre of their cult. They are entered in the
Old Martyrology, and the church is mentioned as
occupied by Montanists at the end of the 4th century.[a]
It may be that the liturgical observance is connected with
the rebuilding of the church by Gregory III (731–41),
but the evidence of the Gradual seems to point to an
earlier date.

July 11. The observance of this day as a feast of
St. Benedict appears in the later books. The day of the
saint's death was March 21; but owing to the clash of this
date with Lent, the Kalendars were slow to admit his
feast on that day. When his relics were translated on
July 11, 623, to S. Benoit-sur-Loire at Fleury, the
opportunity was taken of entering his commemoration
on the translation-day.

On July 23 stands the feast of St. Apollinaris. The
Gradual testifies to its early date, but there is no corresponding entry in Gelasian or **H**. The church or oratory
was founded by Honorius (625–38),[b] and later was appointed as the Station for the Thursday in Passion Week,
when (*c.* 720) the Thursday Stations were instituted. It
stood in close contact with St. Peter's, and the founder
ordered a weekly procession from the church to St.
Peter's to be held on Saturdays.

July 25. Here the first movement towards the extension of the commemoration of the less-known apostles is
seen to be beginning. In the earlier times there was no
cult established of apostles merely on account of their
apostleship; consequently there had been hitherto no
recognition of St. James the Great, SS. Bartholomew,
Thomas, Matthew, Simon and Jude. The defect seems
to have been felt in France, and in the early Gelasian
there is provision for a vigil and a festival of 'All Apostles'.
Some of the Collects are those found in the Leonine for

[a] *L. P.* i. 222, 419, 422.   [b] *L. P.* i. 323, 326.

SS. Peter and Paul. In the Mixed Sacramentaries this provision was mainly transferred to SS. Simon and Jude, October 28; but in the Angoulême Sacramentary it figures also as *Omnium Apostolorum*, at the head of the *Commune sanctorum.*

For St. James recourse was chiefly had to the Masses for SS. Peter and Paul from the earlier Gelasian, and ultimately from the Leonine. In the music-books St. James does not appear till late, and then with borrowed music. SS. Simon and Jude and St. Matthew had gained their entry sooner, and a small amount of special music seems to have been provided for each of these two festivals.

AUGUST

There is a large group of Saints-days which go back to early times.

	1. St. Peter's Chains.	1. Machabees.
2. Stephen.		
6. Sixtus, Felicissimus and Agapitus.		7. Donatus.
8. Cyriac.		
9, 10, 17. Lawrence with Vigil & Octave.		
11. Tiburtius. Susanna.	12. Euplius.	
13. Hippolytus.		
	14. Eusebius.	
		15. Vigil Assumption.
18. Agapitus.		19. Magnus.
	22. Timothy. Symphorian.	24. Bartholomew.
	25. Genesius.	
		27. Rufus.
28. Hermes.		
	29. Sabina.	
	30. Felix and Adauctus.	Decollation Elisha.

[A.] All the martyrs in the left-hand column have their

place in the *Leonianum* except Cyriac, Tiburtius, and Hermes. The Philocalian list includes Sixtus, Felicissimus and Agapitus, Cyriac, Lawrence, and Hippolytus.

Aug. 2. Stephen. In the Leonine (§ xix) all the nine Masses given on this day belong to the Protomartyr, while the day belongs to Pope Stephen who was martyred in 255 and whose name is in the Philocalian lists among the *depositiones episcoporum* and not among the martyrs. The last of the nine Masses speaks of the basilica dedicated in honour of the Protomartyr. This may refer to the church on the *Via Latina* founded by Leo I (440–61) or the famous Stational Church on the Caelian Hill erected by Simplicius (468–83).[a] In the former the feast of Pope Stephen was observed, as is shown by the note *Via Latina* added on this day in some Sacramentaries and Gospel-capitularies. The Leonine suggests that the day of Pope Stephen was used for a feast of the Protomartyr just as the church of the Protomartyr was used for the day of the Pope.

Aug. 6. Sixtus stands alone in the early Gelasian; the Leonine, following the Philocalian Kalendar, follows up a series of Masses for St. Sixtus with one for SS. Felicissimus and Agapitus. The association is more likely to be topographical and liturgical than a mere matter of date, as the cemetery of Callistus, where Sixtus lay, is not far from the cemetery of Praetextatus, the resting-place of the others; and both are on the *Via Appia*.[b]

Aug. 8. Cyriac heads a group of six martyrs recorded in the Philocalian Kalendar but unknown to the Leonine. The martyrs were buried six miles out on the Ostian Road, as the Martyrology records; and a church was built or rebuilt on the spot by Honorius (625–38).[c] But the

---

[a] *L. P.* i. 249; Huelsen, 474.

[b] The Damasine Inscription for Felicissimus and Agapitus (Ihm, 23) was found in 1927. See *Rivista di Arch. Christ.*, vol. iv (1927), pp. 8 and 234–48.

[c] *L. P.* i. 326.

source of the festival is also to be found in the *titulus Cyriaci*, the title-church which had at least since the 5th century existed in Rome by the Baths of Diocletian. Presumably the founder was a Cyriac; and subsequently the martyr Cyriac was brought in to be patron, because of the identity of name; and so the anniversary of the martyr became the church-festival of the *titulus*, and claimed a place in the Kalendar. The Station was held here on XL⁵iii; but it was later transferred to the Deaconry of Cyriac when the *titulus* fell into ruin.[a]

Aug. 10. Lawrence. The Leonine in the 12th of the Masses provides for the vigil, and in the 14th and last it expressly mentions the octave.

In the Gregorian tradition, but not in the Gelasian, two masses were provided for the Day. There were once at St. Lawrence two churches adjacent to one another: they were ultimately fused into one by Honorius III (1216–27).[b]

Aug. 11. Tiburtius is noted in the Old Roman Martyrology as buried *Inter duas lauros* on the *Via Labicana*, that is four miles out. The festival is common to early Gelasian **V** and early Gregorian as shown in the Gospel-lists.

Aug. 13. Hippolytus is the Roman martyr[c] buried in the cemetery called after his name on the *Via Tiburtina*. He is associated in the Philocalian list and also in the *Leonianum* with Pontian, who lay as Pope in the cemetery of Callistus on the *Via Appia*; but Hippolytus alone survived into the later books. The anti-pope thus strangely survived the Pope, but only by losing his identity and being taken for the jailor of St. Lawrence.

Aug. 18. Agapitus has a Mass in the Leonine which has slipped in under the heading of the preceding entry

---

[a] Grisar, *Das Missale*, p. 33.
[b] See Morin's note in *Rev. Bénéd.* xxviii (1911), 312.
[c] Kirsch, 29, 30.

SS. YPOLITI ET PONTIANI. The feast passed into early Gregorian and Gelasian; but, curiously, the Old English Martyrology ascribes it to the New and not to the Old Mass-book.[a] The saint belonged to Palestrina and was buried there, thirty-three miles from Rome: the entry is not in the Early Roman Martyrology.[b] It is not clear how or why it came in sufficiently early to be given a place in both Gelasian and Gregorian. Perhaps the martyr was connected with Pope Agapitus who died at Constantinople on April 22, 536, and was brought home to be buried in St. Peter's, and came into fame then. An oratory had already been built in honour of the martyr close to St. Lawrence by Felix III (483–92),[c] and it was there presumably that the festival was kept.

Aug. 28. Hermes is a martyr entered in the Philo-calian Kalendar as buried in the cemetery of Basilla on the *Via Salaria Vetus*.[d] The feast is not in the *Leonianum*, but is common to early Gelasian and Gregorian; it was presumably kept in a subterranean church there, which dates from Pelagius II (578–90).[e]

[B.] There are four festivals to be taken into account next which are in the early Gregorian tradition, but not in the early Gelasian.

Aug. 14. Eusebius was founder and subsequently patron of the *titulus Eusebii*, and as such he figures in an addition to the Old Roman Martyrology.[f] The church is attested as early as 474. At a later date legend was busy with him and with a Roman priest of that name, martyred and buried in St. Callistus.

Aug. 22. Timothy. The entry is in the Philocalian Kalendar, and correspondingly in the Early Roman Martyrology. The saint, of whom nothing authentic is

---

[a] Above, p. 46.   [b] Kirsch, 209.   [c] *L. P.* i. 252.
[d] Kirsch, 31.   [e] *L. P.* i. 309; Huelsen, 262.
[f] Kirsch, 52, 53, 171, 172; Huelsen, 251.

known, was buried on the Ostian Road. His name no doubt suggested the propriety of his lying near St. Paul. The site has not been identified with any certainty, but the feast was observed *ad S. Paulum* according to some Gospel-books. There is some special music provided for it.

On Gallican soil there was added on this day the commemoration of Symphorian of Autun, martyred *c.* 180. His *acta* are famous, and his reputation was widespread. The addition is found in most of the Gospel-books of the early type, though not in **R**.

Aug. 29. Sabina. This is another case of a feast of a *titulus* and Stational Church which has no place in the Gelasian tradition.[a] The church is well known, but the saint is not. It was built in the 5th century by the priest, Peter,[b] and the tablet recording its foundation is still to be seen in the church. This does not mention the dedication, but the *titulus Sabinae* is mentioned in the signatures of the Synod of 499. Later on, as if further to justify the name, which at the first may have been simply that of a benefactress on whose behalf Peter acted as founder, the relics of a martyred Sabina were translated to the church from the neighbourhood of Terni towards the end of the 7th century.

The feast probably commemorates this translation. It figures in our earliest forms of Gregorian.

Aug. 30. Felix and Adauctus are well known from their shrine in the cemetery of Commodilla, and the epitaph of Pope Damasus.[c] They have no mention in the Philocalian list, but have a set of seven Masses provided for their day in the *Leonianum*, only the first of which is proper to them. The entry is often found on the 29th in place of the 30th.

---

[a] The Old English Martyrology assigns it to the 'New Mass-book'.
[b] *L. P.* i. 235, 236.   [c] Ihm, No. 7; Kirsch, 76.

[C.] There is also a group of feasts to be considered, which are specially Gelasian.

Aug. 15. The Assumption of the B.V.M., like the other feasts of the B.V.M., is part of the Gelasian tradition before it comes into the Gregorian. It is in **V** but not in the early Gregorian. It is absent from the early Epistle-list **We.** The list of days given there is clearly incomplete, and ordinarily it is not to be counted as giving valuable negative evidence. But in this case it is hard to suppose that if this feast had been known to the writer he would have passed it over. In the early Gospel-books the entry seems new and strange; in **Wg** we read *Natale S. Mariae,* in **R** *Solemnia S. Mariae.* Later the former style was dropped, and in the Standard Gospel-books *Solemnia de pausatione Mariae* became common, reflecting the κοίμησις of the Greek title.

Aug. 7. Donatus of Arezzo is found in **V** and Mixed Sacramentaries; his name is entered without comment in the Old English Martyrology.

Aug. 19. Magnus of Anagni is in the same case, except that the O.E. Martyrology comments that the name comes from the Old Mass-book.

Aug. 27. Rufus of Capua is as Magnus.

Aug. 30. The Decollation of St. John Baptist. Where the early Gregorian has Felix and Adauctus the Gelasian **V** has the *Passio* of the Baptist, an entry which appears in the list of feasts observed by Perpetuus, Bishop of Tours (461–91).[a] Under the title *Decollatio* the two were combined quite early in the history, so that the joint entry is found even in Gospel-books of the earlier type. The addition was in early times made on the Gelasian day, the 29th, and not, as above, on the 30th. There is added also on the 30th in some early Capitularies, though not

---

[a] See Gregory of Tours, *Hist. Francorum,* x. 31, list of vigils. It comes in the list, however, between Pentecost and the feast of SS. Peter and Paul.

in the Standard Gregorian Gospel-books, a *Depositio Elisaei propheti*. The former addition held its ground, while the latter did not. It is said that the tomb of the prophet was a venerated shrine until it was destroyed by Julian the Apostate.[a] The Eastern Church holds the festival on June 14; no such commemoration became prominent in the West until the rise of the Carmelites, who in 1399 adopted the festival.

Aug. 1. The early Kalendar contained no entry for this day, though it is probable that it was kept locally as the dedication festival of the *titulus Eudoxiae*, the church of the apostles and specially of St. Peter on the Esquiline, built under Sixtus III (432–40) and renowned for its relics of St. Peter's chains. The Stational Mass was held there, from the 7th century at least, on a number of days; and there the relics were venerated of the Seven Machabees, whose festival fell on August 1.[b] These heroes obtained liturgical observance first. Their Mass is found in the early Gelasian; but its Roman origin is clear from the Leonine prayers embodied therein. The church was rebuilt by Hadrian (772–95); and thereafter the festival of the Chains appears, ousting to a large extent the Machabees in the Gelasian books, and borrowing its music from elsewhere.

Aug. 24. Bartholomew is one of the group of added Apostles that appears first in the Mixed Sacramentaries.

[D.] A small further group contains additions which are made in a few of the early Gregorian authorities, but are principally in evidence in the Standard Gospel-books.

Aug. 11. Susanna. This feast appears only to disappear again. It is the feast of one of the Roman *tituli*, like Eusebius and Sabina above; and the Station was held

---

[a] Stadler, *Heiligenlexicon*, Elisha.

[b] Syrian Martyrologies; and thence taken into the Old Roman, and Carthaginian (Mabillon, *Vet. Anal.*, iii. 398). Cp. Kirsch, 165. For the connexion with St. Felicitas, see pp. 178 and 141.

there on XL³vii. Its original name is the *titulus Susannae* (or *Gaii*) *ad duas domos*, and it figures in the signatures of the Council of 499. The full style as given in the Early Martyrology is *ad duas domos juxta Diocletianas*.[a]

A new prominence was given to the church in the time of Sergius (687–701) who had been priest of the church.[b] He became a generous benefactor to it, and the benefactions were recorded on a marble tablet of which the greater part survives.

The entrance of this feast upon the Kalendar perhaps belongs to this date. But the history repeated itself in 795 when Leo III, another priest of the church,[c] became Pope; and more probably the brief career of St. Susanna as a liturgical feast begins from the later period, for it is unknown as late as the *Hadrianum*.

Aug. 12. Euplius. The fame of this victim of the Diocletian persecution rests chiefly on the fact that the genuine *Acta* of his martyrdom at Catania have been preserved.[d] There seems to have been a period of interest in him during the 7th and 8th centuries, which brought his name into the Kalendar for a transient period. An oratory was built in his honour by Theodore (642–9) and restored by Hadrian (772–95).[e] The entry is unusual in the early Gospel-books, but occurs in **Wg**. This fact points to the earlier date as being the time when it began.

Aug. 25. Genesius. This is a similar case of a martyr of whom a genuine *Passio* has been preserved.[f] Genesius the Roman player, martyr in 286, has been much confused with Genesius of Arles, a more shadowy figure, whose *Passio* was written by Bishop Paulinus,[g] and both August 24 and 25 are involved in the confusion.[h] The earlier forms of the Roman Martyrology seem to know

---

[a] Kirsch, 75.   [b] *L. P.* i. 371, 377, 380.   [c] *L. P.* ii. 3.
[d] Printed in Ruinart, *Acta Sincera Martyrum. B. H. L.* 2728.
[e] *L. P.* i. 333, 334, 508.   [f] See Ruinart, *ut s., B. H. L.* 3315.
[g] *B. H. L.* 3304.   [h] Kirsch, 173–6.

neither, the latter to know both. The tradition is probably a literary one, not a liturgical one.

An oratory dedicated to Genesius the martyr existed in Rome probably in the 7th century, as it was repaired by Gregory III (731–41).[a] The feast is found in the Standard Gospel-books as also in one or two of the earlier type.[b]

SEPTEMBER

1. Priscus.

	8. Hadrian.	Nativity of B.V.M.
		9. Gorgonius.
	11. Protus and Hyacinth.	
14. Cornelius & Cyprian.		14. Holy Cross.
	15. Nicomede.	
16. Euphemia. Lucy and Geminian.		
		20. Eustace.
		21. Matthew.
	27. Cosmas and Damian.	
29. Michaelmas.		

[A.] Three of the above mentioned are in the *Leonianum*, those on the 14th, 16th, and 29th.

Sept. 14. Cyprian is commemorated on the day of his martyrdom in the Philocalian Kalendar. The date of the death of his contemporary, Pope Cornelius, was apparently not known; the Philocalian list does not contain it. So his commemoration was joined to that of Cyprian, possibly by St. Leo,[c] who built a church in his honour at the place of his burial in the cemetery of Callistus. The Philocalian Kalendar directed the commemoration of St. Cyprian to take place in that cemetery. Thus Cornelius provided the place, and Cyprian the date.

[a] *L. P.* i. 419.   [b] Pf. Py.   [c] *L. P.* i. 239.

I

Sept. 16. Euphemia. This is the Roman date, as contrasted with the Eastern date (see above, April 13) found in the Gelasian. The *Leonianum*, besides three Masses for St. Euphemia, has also a Preface, which has been placed too early in the middle of a Mass of SS. Cornelius and Cyprian.

The fame of St. Euphemia in the West was due to the fact that the Council of Chalcedon (451) was held in a church dedicated to her. It is not clear how early any church of St. Euphemia was built in Rome. There was such a church, situated near St. Pudentiana, which is first attested through being repaired by Sergius (687–701) after lying long unroofed.[a] With this building was probably connected the claim that her relics were brought from the East to Rome in 617. The feast of September 16 is probably the dedication feast of this Roman church (see above, p. 100).

Sept. 16. Lucy and Geminian. Combined with this is the feast of the Roman martyr, St. Lucy, without or with her companion, St. Geminian. The church of this St. Lucy lay not far from St. Euphemia's, and the proximity of the two churches to one another was probably the reason for the combination. The founder was Honorius (625–38),[b] and the epithet *in Orphea* or *in silice* was added in order to distinguish this from other churches called after a St. Lucy. These two saints do not appear in the Early Martyrology; their entry into fame was probably due to the composition of their *Passio*.[c] The entry in the early Capitularies is SS. Lucy and Euphemia.

Sept. 29.[d] Michaelmas is the dedication of the basilica on the *Via Salaria* (as the *Leonianum* specifies) seven miles from the city. There is no record of its foundation, little of its history, and no trace of it survives. Two churches of later date lying within the city presumably

---

[a] *L. P.* i. 375, 380.   [b] *L. P.* i. 324, 326.   [c] *B. H. L.* 4985.
[d] The date is wrongly given in the *Leonianum* as Prid. Kal. Oct.

superseded the suburban church when it disappeared; one enlarged by Symmachus (498–514)[a] and the chapel in the mausoleum of Hadrian established in the 7th century.

[B.] One further entry is common to early Gelasian and Gregorian.

Sept. 27. Cosmas and Damian. A church dedicated to this famous pair of saints from Cilicia was set up by Felix IV (526–30)[b] on the site of secular public buildings placed on the *Via Sacra*. A Station was held there on the Sunday before their festival, according to directions given in the earlier Gospel-books but not in the later ones; and also on the Second Sunday after Easter. A quarter of a century earlier the cult was already established, for Symmachus (498–514) built at St. Mary's[c] an oratory dedicated to these saints. Presumably it was during this period that their names were inserted in the Canon of the Mass.

[C.] Turning now to the early Gregorian tradition we note as follows:

Sept. 8. Hadrian. The transformation of the old Senate-house into a church of St. Hadrian took place under Honorius (625–38).[d] The absence of the entry from the Gelasian may be due to the fact that the feast of the Nativity of the B.V. Mary was already there in possession of the day. Later the day was claimed in Gregorian circles also for this feast of Our Lady; but the commemoration of St. Hadrian maintained its position in the earliest Gradual, even when it had surrendered and taken a subordinate place in the Sacramentary.

Sept. 11. Protus and Hyacinth. These are old Roman martyrs recorded in the Philocalian Kalendar and the Early Martyrology[e] as lying in the cemetery of Basilla,

[a] *L. P.* i. 262; Grisar, 108.   [b] *L. P.* i. 279.   [c] Ibid. i. 262.
[d] Ibid. i. 324, 326.   [e] Kirsch, 32.

or Hermes, on the *Via Salaria Vetus* not far from the city. It is said that Damasus recovered their bodies after they had been hidden during the persecution of Diocletian, and replaced them with an inscription. A second inscription, discovered in 1845, speaks of the Priest Theodore as the restorer of their shrines; and epigraphy makes it unlikely that in this case either the poem or the tablet is due to Damasus, though it is not much later in date. Another epigram in their honour was set up by Symmachus (498–514).[a] There is no sign of liturgical observance earlier than the Gospel-books, and the musical evidence does not suggest an early date for the acceptance of the festival into the Kalendar. The inscriptions, however, suggest a popular cult.

Sept. 15. Nicomede. The entry refers not to the *titulus* called *Nicomedis*[b] or *Matthaei*, which is probably to be identified with the *titulus* called later that of SS. Marcellinus and Peter, but to the Roman martyr who gave his name to the cemetery on the *Via Nomentana*. His name is not in the Philocalian list nor in the Early Martyrology.

The suspicion arises that possibly the cemetery had originally a connexion with the *titulus* and the same founder, in which case this person, a martyred St. Nicomede, was an afterthought, notwithstanding the *Passio*, which in due course was provided for him.

At any rate, Boniface V (619–25) *perfecit cymiterium S. Nicomedi et dedicavit eum*;[c] and the feast probably so arose. The music for the day is mainly borrowed from St. Lawrence.

---

[a] Ihm, Nos. 49, 96, 97.

[b] The term is only known from the signatures of the Roman Council in 499, and from a tombstone of the 5th century found near the *Ambo* in St. Lawrence outside the walls. Kirsch, *Titelkirchen*, pp. 56–7. It apparently superseded the *titulus Matthaei*, a church which does not appear as a *titulus* after 499, and has now perished. Huelsen, 386.

[c] *L. P.* i. 321, 322.

[D.] The Gelasian festivals are of interest.

Sept. 1. Priscus is a saint of Capua as already noted above (p. 42 &c).

Sept. 9. Gorgonius is a Roman martyr entered in the Philocalian list and the Old Martyrology as lying in his own cemetery at the place called *inter duas lauros* on the *Via Labicana.*[a] The cemetery is now usually called after SS. Peter and Marcellinus; the tomb has not been identified. In spite of a Damasine inscription[b] the feast fell outside the stream of tradition, not being accepted (for some reason unknown) into the Gregorian documents.

More favour waited upon two others.

Sept. 8. Nativity of the B.V. Mary. This passed, like the rest of the feasts of the B.V.M., from Greek sources into the Gelasian, and thence through the later Gregorian into the general stream. It is not in the earlier Gospel-books, but is in the Standard-type, side by side with St. Hadrian (above). The music appears late in the Gradual and is borrowed, but there is a good special office in the Antiphonal, formed for the most part on old themes.

Sept. 14. Exaltation of the Holy Cross. This has a similar history: it came from Greek sources into the early Gelasian, but not into the early Gregorian. The feast clashed with that of SS. Cornelius and Cyprian, but it succeeded in establishing itself side by side in the later Gregorian books. The music provided in the Gradual is partly borrowed from the *Temporale* and partly new, but the new is not of a classical order.

[E.] A further addition is found in the later Gregorian—the Standard Gospel-capitulary.

Sept. 20. Eustace. This feast possibly came in through the founding of a hospital under the saint's patronage by Stephen III (752–7).[c] Even before this foundation there had been on this spot (called *in platana*) a deaconry,

[a] Kirsch, 31.   [b] Ihm, No. 31.   [c] *L. P.* i. 440, 456.

which is mentioned in two documents of Gregory II (715–31).[a]

Sept. 21. St. Matthew is among the group of Apostles brought into the Mixed Sacramentaries, usually with a vigil. The church called *Matthaei* which was at one time a *titulus*[b] seems to have left no mark on the early Kalendar.

OCTOBER

7 Mark.   Marcellus and
                               Apuleius.
14 Callistus.

18 Luke.
25 Chrysanthus
     and Daria.
28 Simon and
     Jude.

[A.] This month contains the entries of two popes, on the 7th Mark, and on the 14th Callistus. They are absent from the early Gelasian tradition, which has on October 7 only Marcellus and Apuleius.

Oct. 7. Pope Mark (336) built two churches each called after his name;[c] in the cemeterial one he was buried; the urban one became the *titulus Marci*, where the Station was held on Monday in the third week of Lent.

Oct. 14. Callistus, whose deposition is entered on the Philocalian Kalendar, is associated with the church of St. Mary in Trastevere which is the *titulus* called *Iulii* or *Callisti*. This was one of the churches built by Julius (337–52),[d] and he built a cemeterial church also *ad Callistum*.

[B.] The Gelasian has in October only SS. Marcellus and Apuleius who belong to the Capuan group of saints inscribed there (above p. 42).

Two noteworthy additions, found in the Mixed Sacra-

---

[a] Kehr, i. 97.   [b] Above, p. 132[b].
[c] *L. P.* i. 202–3.   [d] *L. P.* i. 9, 141, 205, 206.

mentaries, are biblical,—St. Luke (18th), and SS. Simon and Jude (28th) preceded by a vigil. The material of the latter is chiefly drawn from the services *Omnium Apostolorum* in the early Gelasian (p. 39), but some of the music is new.

[C.] Oct. 25. SS. Chrysanthus and Daria are sometimes found here in the Gospel-books; sometimes Chrysanthus, Maurus, and Daria figure with Saturninus on November 29, as in the *Gelasianum* also. In the Martyrology they appear in another form on August 12. The last entry seems to depend directly upon the *Passio Chrysanthi et Dariae*, and so to have no liturgical significance. The entry in November is probably due to the fact that that day was unquestionably the feast of St. Saturninus, as the Philocalian list shows; and it was convenient to combine with that feast the commemoration of these other martyrs who lay close by on the *Via Salaria Vetus*. The October date was the day of the translation which took place in 844; but that day was probably chosen for it as being one already associated with the saints.[a]

NOVEMBER

1. Caesarius.	
8. Quatuor Coronati.	
	9. Theodore.
	11. Mennas.
	12. Martin.
21. Cecilia.	
23. Clement, Felicitas.	
24. Chrysogonus.	
29. Saturninus, Vigil of Andrew.	Chrysanthus, Maurus, and Daria.
30. Andrew.	

[A.] This is the full list in the Gospel-books for this month, and there is something to be said in every case for the supposition that each name figured in the groundwork Kalendar.

[a] Kirsch, 38, 90–3. *AA. SS.*, Oct. xi. 490; and see further below, p. 142.

The *Leonianum* has the entries of the 8th, 21st, 23rd (both saints), 24th, 29th, and 30th, and implies a Vigil of St. Andrew. The Gelasian has the 8th, 21st with a vigil, 23rd (both saints), and 29th.

Nov. 1. Caesarius is connected with the little oratory of the Palace, situated on the Palatine, and therefore a place of some distinction. It is attested as early as 603, but there is no evidence of liturgical importance before that of these Gospel-books. The Sacramentaries from Hadrian onwards specially record that there is a *Collecta* at SS. Cosmas and Damian before the Mass and give the required Collect. This is no doubt a recognition of its civil importance. Caesarius was a martyr of Terracina whose local feast was April 21.[a] His relics were brought in the time of Valentinian III (423–55) to the imperial chapel; and this feast of November 1 probably commemorates the dedication.[b] This procedure illustrates the custom of adopting for churches as patron some saint with a suitable name. Caesarius was suitable for the ancient palace of the Caesars.

The chapel itself disappeared, and its disappearance made it all the easier to change the observance of the day to another purpose. So All Saints in the 9th century superseded Caesarius, and a monastery[c] succeeded to the oratory.

It has already been told at May 13 how the Pantheon was dedicated to St. Mary and all martyrs (probably 609); and this dedication became the type of future dedication services. It also pointed the way to the feast of All Saints.

Already Bede in his *Chronicle* connects this dedication of the church with a feast of All Saints (not 'all Martyrs'), and this passage was copied continually for November 1,

[a] *L. P.* i. 371, 378. Kirsch, 182, 208; Gregory, *Epist.* xiii. 1. Huelsen, p. 234, places it in the Lateran Palace, but this is not consistent with the *Collecta*.
[b] Lanzoni, i. 148 treats April 21 as the Roman date: but the liturgical evidence shows the contrary.   [c] Huelsen, 232.

by later writers, especially by the martyrologies,[a] so that it became a tradition that these feasts in some way hung together.[b]

But there was no substantial connexion between the two. The service of May 13 was quite unsuited to November 1, and, in fact, did not contribute to it. It concerned itself largely with the church itself, as the Introit *Terribilis est locus iste* at once shows ; the rest followed suit. The All-Saints-day services, on the contrary, borrowed existing music from various festivals of martyrs. When once the feast began, it had an Epistle and Gospel of their own, while the Dedication Service took the Gospel of the Sunday.

So far as Service-books are concerned the All-Saints-day services do not seem to be included in those of the 9th century.

The dating, then, of the festival of All Saints is important, and it is difficult to reach from Kalendars. However, there is one which gives definite evidence of the observance of the day in England by the middle of the 8th century. This is the pseudo-Bede Martyrology, written in hexameters shortly after the death of Bede. It is a Kalendar rather than a Martyrology proper, for its interest is not hagiological or literary, but strictly liturgical. With the Saints-days are interwoven the obits of the first six archbishops of York, ending with Egbert who died in 767. The original document, therefore, may be dated with confidence between 767 and 780—the date of the death of Egbert's successor. It is preserved in several forms[c] as the result of omissions or additions; the additions mainly concern local saints, and the omissions are chiefly due to a waning interest in the peculiar features of the Kalendar which belong to York or Yorkshire,

[a] See Florus, in Quentin, p. 370, and Ado, ibid. 636.
[b] See the remarks of Beleth, *Rationale*, 127, in *P. L.* CCII.
[c] A critical text is given in Quentin, pp. 123–6.

including the Dedication Festival which is entered on
April 27. The entry on November 1 is, however, common to all the forms, and runs thus:

> Multiplici rutilet gemma ceu in fronte November
> cunctorum fulget sanctorum laude decorus.

It apparently implies the observance of All Saints' Day
on that date.

This seems to suggest that November 1 is to be identified as the probable date of the dedication of the chapel
or oratory of All Saints in St. Peter's by Gregory III
(731–41); and that the observance of All Saints' Day, at
any rate in England, derives from that dedication. Another century passed before Gregory IV urged the
observance of the feast on Louis the Pious, and the
Empire adopted it in 835; and meanwhile the day had
not been generally kept. Its general diffusion then
belongs to the middle of the 9th century.[a]

Nov. 8. *Quatuor Coronati.* In the Philocalian Kalendar there is an entry on the 9th, *Clementis, Semproniani,
Claudi, Nicostrati in comitatum*; and there is an echo of this
in the Old Martyrology *Romae Clementis et Simproni.*
Also on the 8th the Martyrology[b] has *Romae ad Celio
monte Natale Simforiani Claudi Nicostrati et Castoris.*
Here is a discrepancy not only in the date, but in one
name of the group, and in the place. The entries presumably are not duplicates but alternatives. This group
of *Quatuor Coronati* was buried *in comitatum*, that is by
the Guards' barracks in the cemetery, known as *inter
duas lauros* or Peter and Marcellinus, on the *Via Labicana*. They were said to be four Roman sculptors
martyred in Pannonia under Galerius.

The *titulus Aemilianae* on the Caelian hill was dedicated
to them in the 6th century,[c] perhaps with a translation

---

[a] See Ado, *Martyrology*, ad loc., and Sigebert, *Chron.*, at 835 (*P. L.* CLX. 159).
[b] Kirsch, 35.
[c] Between the synod of 499 and that of 595, to judge by the signatures.

of relics. Thus the date of the original Deposition differs from that of the festival of the church; and it is the latter which came into the Kalender.

The difference in the names is less easily explained. The *Leonianum* is not definite as to date, nor does it commit itself as to the names. The early Gelasian gives *Costiani Claudi Castori Simproniani* in the title, and no names in the prayers. Hadrian gives in the first prayer five names—Claudius, Nicostratus, Simphronianus, Castorius, and Simplicius. Excavations have revealed in the appropriate site a staircase leading to two chambers, in one of which was found a graffito *Sc'e Cle*. This probably refers to the first name on the cemetery list which has disappeared from the church list in favour of Castor. Kirsch suggests that possibly the Clement was omitted in the church dedication in order to avoid confusion with the neighbouring church of St. Clement; and Castor taken from the same spot in the cemetery to fill the place.

Nov. 9. The claim of St. Theodore to a place in the early form of Kalendars is doubtful. The date is that of the Eastern martyr St. Theodore of Amasea in Pontus, whose cult was widespread. But the festival is absent from the early Gelasian. As in the case of other non-Roman saints, it is necessary to depend mainly upon ecclesiological evidence.

The existing church in the *Velabrum*[a] is built on the foundations of a circular secular building, probably a temple. In the apse is a mosaic of the same epoch as the mosaic in SS. Cosmas and Damian erected by Felix IV (526). In each of them St. Theodore appears. In each church the same plan is observable of adapting a round temple for Christian worship. It may fairly be conjectured that St. Theodore's church owes its origin to Felix, or dates approximately to his time.

But *L. P.* i. 324 ascribes the building and dedication of a church in their honour to Honorius (625–38).   [a] Marucchi, 245, 356.

An earlier church of St. Theodore[a] had existed, perhaps in the same neighbourhood, which is mentioned in
418; but it disappeared. Some connexion between this
and the later church of St. Theodore is possible; but, so
far as documents are concerned, nothing clear is known
of the church till it appears as a *diaconia* in the time of
Leo III (795–816), a date too late to be of interest for
this purpose.

The music is all borrowed and is used without uni-
formity, and this fact confirms the surmise that the entry
is not an early one in the Kalendar.

Nov. 11. Mennas the Egyptian martyr had a church,
situated some little way out on the Ostian Road, as early
as the days of St. Gregory. The 35th of his Homilies on
the Gospel was pronounced there on the anniversary of
the martyr's death;[b] but the Gospel read was Luke
xxi. 9–19, not Luke ix. 23–7, as now given in the
Gospel-books. The church seems to have been the home
of an Alexandrian guild. It has long since vanished.
The fact that it has music of its own confirms the Gregorian date; and the fact that it is not in the Gelasian is
some evidence that the Gelasian is pre-Gregorian. It is
noteworthy that on this day also is the festival of Mennas,
the hermit of Samnium, whose life St. Gregory sketched
in one of his dialogues.[c] Curiously enough on both occasions he spoke of the two kinds of martyrdom, one in act
and the other in mind, one public, the other hidden;—as
if the name Mennas brought up the same set of ideas
to his thought.

Nov. 11, 12. St. Martin's fame (d. 399) spread to
Rome so that a century after his death Symmachus
(498–514) added a chapel dedicated in his honour to the

---

[a] *L. P.* ii. 12, 41.
[b] *L. P.* ii. 34: *P. L.* LXXVI. 1259. It begins 'Quia longior ab urbe digressi
sumus'.
[c] *Dial.* iii. 26. *P. L.* LXXVII. 280.

titulus Equitii which Silvester (314–35) had founded,[a] and which was later called *titulus Silvestri*. Later St. Martin's name was added as well, and in the end this alone survived. The festival found no place in the Leonine nor in the early Gelasian. It came into the early Gregorian apparently after St. Mennas; for at first it was not kept on the 11th, the day of his burial, but was postponed to the 12th probably because St. Mennas was already in possession. This evidence points to a comparatively late date for the entry of the festival into the Kalendar. The music-books confirm this view; for the mass-music is not uniformly used and it is all borrowed. The Office in the Antiphonal belongs to the Silver Age.

Nov. 21. St. Cecilia. Five Masses are given in the *Leonianum*, but there is none for a vigil as is the case in the Gelasian. The church is an ancient *titulus*.

Nov. 23. St. Clement has four Masses and St. Felicitas two in the *Leonianum*; while a seventh Mass combines the two, and plays upon their names. Allusion is made to the sons of St. Felicitas in all the three last. See above p. 117.

In the case of Felicitas[b] the festival is probably due to her 'deposition', which was in the cemetery called after Maximus or after herself. In Clement's case there was no early tradition or record of the date of his death and burial in exile. The Philocalian lists are silent about him, as about all popes previous to the 3rd century. Consequently his association with this day may be due only to his having been adopted as patron of the *titulus Clementis*, perhaps in the 4th century; and the day may be the festival of that ancient church.

Felicitas overflowed on to other dates not only in the Martyrology but in the Kalendar;[c] but this is her proper day. Archaeological evidence confirms the early date ascribed to her cult. Boniface I (418–22) built an oratory

---

[a] *L. P.* i. 40.   [b] Kirsch, 89.   [c] Above, pp. 118, 127.

over her tomb;[a] and a chapel of the 6th century was discovered in 1812 in which she was depicted with her
reputed Seven Sons.[b]

Nov. 24. St. Chrysogonus. In this case, more certainly than on the preceding day, the festival has its origin
in an urban church not in a suburban *martyrium.*[c] The
ancient *titulus Chrysogoni* became associated with St.
Chrysogonus of Aquileia, and probably took the date of
his *natale* as its church-festival.[d] Like other non-Roman
saints such as Theodore, Mennas, and Martin, this saint
had no place in the Gelasian, but belonged purely to the
city of Rome. In the *Leonianum* the Mass has no reference to any named martyrs, while the heading gives
SS. Chrysogonus and Gregory. No satisfactory explanation has been found of this mention of Gregory here.
The name of Chrysogonus is in the Canon of the Mass.

Nov. 29. Saturninus is entered in the Philocalian
Kalendar and the Old Martyrology. A basilica covered
his grave in the cemetery of Thrason on the Via Salaria.[e]
It was burnt down in the time of Felix IV (526–30) and
that pope rebuilt it.

The older Gelasian commemorates with Saturninus[f]
a trio of Roman martyrs, Chrysanthus, Maurus, and
Daria, and this is not merely a martyrological addition,
for there some mention is made of Chrysanthus in the
prayers. The interest taken in Rome about these saints
is early, for Damasus set up two inscriptions in honour
of them, one for Chrysanthus and Daria and the other for
Maurus.[g] The relation of these saints to October 25 has
been already discussed at that date (p. 135).

Nov. 30. Andrew. Four Masses are provided in the
Leonianum, one of which is meant for the Vigil. The

---

[a] *L. P.* i. 327.   [b] See above, p. 117, and Huelsen, 252.   [c] Kirsch, 182.
[d] The converse may be true; but the Early Martyrology gives the date for
him at Aquileia, and the mention of Rome seems to be later.
[e] *L. P.* i. 279, 280.   [f] Kirsch, 91–3.   [g] Ihm, 87 and 44.

ancient church of St. Andrew in Rome was that called
cata Barbara which was founded in the time of Pope
Simplicius (468–83).[a]

DECEMBER

7. Octave of Andrew.
11. Damasus.

13. Lucy.

21. Thomas.
25. Anastasia.

[A.] The Würzburg Gospel-book is incomplete, and
ends at the Vigil of Andrew. The Reims book contains
only St. Lucy (13th) before it ends with the Vigil of
Christmas. In the Gelasian there is an Octave of Andrew
(7th) and a festival of St. Thomas (21st). The Mixed
Sacramentaries add Damasus on December 11 which the
Philocalian Kalendar marks as the day of the pope's
'deposition'.

Dec. 13. Lucy of Syracuse is different from the Lucy
of Rome, commemorated on September 16 with Geminian. To the Sicilian virgin was dedicated the church of
S. Lucia in septem vias or *iuxta septa solis*, an ancient
church, not archaeologically attested until the time of
Leo III (795–816),[b] but mentioned by the Einsiedeln
Pilgrim in the 8th century.[c] Her cult in Rome goes back
to much earlier days, for she has a place among the
virgins whose names are recited in the Canon of the Mass.
Otherwise the earliest liturgical attestation is that of the
Gospel-books (p. 72).

Dec. 25. The Philocalian list of depositions of martyrs
begins with 'Natus Christus in Betleem Iudeae', and the
habit of beginning the year with Christmas prevails in all
the early Gospel-books. The Gelasian Sacramentary and
the Gelasian Capitularies begin with the Vigil, as do the
later Gospel-lists. The *Leonianum*, however, in December
has Christmas (and a Vigil Mass) at the end of the year,

[a] Huelsen, p. 179.   [b] *L. P.* ii. 11.   [c] Huelsen, p. 305.

followed by St. John Evangelist, and Holy Innocents. In the heading of December 25 it adds the martyr Pastor Basileus Jovian Victorinus Eugenia Felicitas and Anastasia; but no further reference is made to any of them in the nine Masses which follow. This addition comes, in an abbreviated and compressed form, from the Old Roman Martyrology.[a] Of the four men little is known, except that Basileus and Jovian were said to be buried on the *Via Latina.* The three women form a separate group. Eugenia was a Roman martyr buried in the catacomb of Apronianus on the *Via Latina*, as the Martyrology records; Felicitas is there said to belong to Milan. Anastasia is entered as the martyr of Sirmium. Her fame came to Rome from Constantinople whither her relics had been translated in the middle of the 6th century, and placed in view of her name in the church of the Anastasis (Resurrection).

At Rome the *titulus Anastasiae* went back to the time of Damasus (366–84);[b] as in other cases the name was originally, one must suppose, that of the foundress.[c] The position of the church at the foot of the Palatine was probably the reason for its adoption as the Station of the second of the three Masses of Christmas Day. When the saint of Sirmium was brought in as patroness she was given liturgical honours *pari passu* with the Nativity. Accordingly in the Gregorian a Collect, Secret, Preface, and Postcommunion are provided for each. But the Lectionaries show no sign of any duplication of Epistle or Gospel. This custom still is maintained.

The festival of St. Anastasia in the East is not kept on this date, and the difference of date confirms the suggestion that the *titulus* and perhaps the Station, too, preceded the adoption of the saint as patroness of the church.

[a] Kirsch, 43–5.   [b] Huelsen, 172.

[c] This seems more probable than the theory that the church in Rome was originally called 'Anastasis'—church of the Resurrection. Such a name is more Byzantine than Roman.

INDEXES

1 of Authorities; 2 of Abbreviations; 3 of Service-Books; 4 of Places; 5 of Saints and their churches. An asterisk shows a reference to another of the Indexes: the thick figures show the more important references.

1 INDEX OF AUTHORITIES

2 INDEX OF ABBREVIATIONS

3 INDEX OF SERVICE-BOOKS

5 INDEX OF SAINTS AND THEIR CHURCHES
with other personal names

THE ALCUIN CLUB

Founded with the object of promoting the study of the History and Use of the Book of Common Prayer.

President

The Right Rev. CHARLES GORE, D.D.

Vice-Presidents

*The Very Rev. A. S. DUNCAN-JONES, B.D.
*The Rev. F. E. BRIGHTMAN, D.D.
The Rev Canon T. A. LACEY, D.D.
The Rev. Canon C. WORDSWORTH, M.A.

Committee

ATHELSTAN RILEY, Esq., Sr., M.A., F.S.A., *Chairman.*

The Very Rev. A. S. DUNCAN-JONES, B.D.
Chairman of Publications Sub-Committee.

W. H. R. BLACKING, Esq., M.S.A.
Sir CYRIL S. COBB, K.B.E., M.V.O.
*The Rev. PERCY DEARMER, D.D.
The Rev. D. C. DUNLOP, M.A.
F. C. EELES, Esq., F.S.A.Scot.
*The Right Rev. W. H. FRERE, D.D.
*STEPHEN GASELEE, Esq., C.B.E., F.S.A.
HAROLD C. KING, Esq., M.A.
VIVIAN H. KING, Esq., A.R.I.B.A.

The Rev. J. N. NEWLAND-SMITH, M.A.
The Rev. JOCELYN PERKINS, D.C.L., F.R.Hist.S., F.S.A., Sacrist of Westminster Abbey.
*The Rev. Canon J. H. SRAWLEY, D.D., Chancellor of Lincoln Cathedral.
Miss WARD.
*The Rev. Canon R. M. WOOLLEY, D.D.
*E. G. P. WYATT, Esq., M.A.

*Publications Sub-Committee.

Hon. Secretary

E. G. P. WYATT, Esq.
White House, Rustington, Littlehampton.

Hon. Treasurer

VIVIAN H. KING, Esq., A.R.I.B.A.

Acting-Treasurer

Miss WARD
46 Stanley Gardens, South Hampstead, London, N.W. 3.

Bankers

BARCLAYS BANK, 55 England's Lane, London, N.W. 3.

THE ALCUIN CLUB exists in order to encourage and assist in the practical study of ceremonial, and the arrangement of Churches, their furniture and ornaments, in accordance with the rubrics of the Book of Common Prayer, strict obedience to which is the guiding principle of the work of the Club.

The Club shall consist of Members and Associates, to be elected by the Committee.

The Subscription for *Members* shall be 20s. per annum, entitling them to current publications *gratis*; and for *Associates*, 5s. per annum, entitling them to such of the Tracts *gratis* as the Committee may determine. There shall be no Entrance Fee, nor Composition for Subscriptions.

Application for election and for the List of Publications should be sent to Miss WARD, 46 Stanley Gardens, South Hampstead, London, N.W. 3, as well as all Subscriptions.

PUBLICATIONS

COLLECTIONS

I. **English Altars.** A large folio volume with 14 pp. of Collotypes. Explanatory Notes by Sir W. H. St. JOHN HOPE, Litt.D., D.C.L. [*Out of print.*]

II. **Exposition de la Messe.** A large folio volume containing a Treatise on the Mass from a French Version of the Legenda Aurea of Jacobus de Voragine, now in the Fitzwilliam Museum at Cambridge, and 22 plates from Illustrations in this MS. Together with four Tracts from ' The Lay Folks' Mass Book ', ' Merita Missæ ', &c. Edited by the Right Rev. WALTER HOWARD FRERE, D.D. Price £1 10s. [*Out of print.*]

III and IV. **Pontifical Services,** vols. i and ii. Two large folio volumes containing Descriptive Notes and a Liturgical Introduction by the Right Rev. WALTER HOWARD FRERE, D.D., and 20 plates of 62 Illustrations from Miniatures of the fifteenth and sixteenth centuries. Price £1 10s. each. [*Out of print.*]

V. **Dat Boexken van der Missen.** (The Booklet of the Mass.) By GHERIT VANDER GOUDE, 1507. 34 woodcuts illustrating the Celebration of the Holy Communion, described, and the explanatory text of the Flemish original translated, with illustrative excerpts from contemporary missals and tracts by the Rev. PERCY DEARMER, D.D. Price £1 1s. [*Out of print.*]

VI. **The Edwardian Inventories for Bedfordshire.** Edited by F. C. EELES, F.R.Hist.S., F.S.A.Scot., from transcripts by the Rev. J. E. BROWN, B.A. Price 5s.

VII. **The Edwardian Inventories for Huntingdonshire.** Edited by Mrs. S. C. LOMAS, Editor of ' State Papers Charles I Addenda ', &c., from transcripts by T. CRAIB. Price 10s.

VIII. **Pontifical Services,** vol. iii. Descriptive Notes and 143 Illustrations from woodcuts in pontificals of the sixteenth century. Edited by F. C. EELES, F.R.Hist.S., F.S.A.Scot. £1 1s.

IX. **The Edwardian Inventories for Buckinghamshire.** Edited by F. C. EELES, F.R.Hist.S., F.S.A.Scot., from transcripts by the Rev. J. E. BROWN, B.A. Price £1 1s. [*Out of print.*]

X. **Fifty Pictures of Gothic Altars.** Descriptive Notes and 50 Illustrations. Edited by the Rev. PERCY DEARMER, D.D. Price £1 1s. [*Out of print.*]*

XI. **The Sarum Missal in English.** Two volumes, containing a translation of the complete Sarum Missal by the Rev. F. E. WARREN, B.D., F.S.A. Price £1 2s. 6d. [*Out of print.*]

XII. **Pontifical Services,** vol. iv. Descriptive Notes and 134 Illustrations from woodcuts in pontificals of the sixteenth century. Edited by ATHELSTAN RILEY, F.S.A. £1 1s. [*Out of print.*]

* This work has been reprinted by Messrs. Mowbray, and can be purchased by members of the Club on application to the Secretary.

XIII. **A History of the Use of Incense in Divine Worship.** xx +404 pp. 60 Illustrations. By E. G. CUTHBERT F. ATCHLEY, L.R.C.P., M.R.C.S. Price £3.

XIV. **Visitation Articles and Injunctions of the Period of the Reformation,** vol. i. An Introduction on the theory, history, and practice of Episcopal and other Visitations. By the Right Rev. WALTER HOWARD FRERE, D.D. Price £1. [*Out of print.*]

XV. **The Same,** vol. ii (1536–58). Edited by the Right Rev. W. H. FRERE, D.D., with the assistance of W. M. KENNEDY, Litt.D. Price 30s. [*Out of print.*]

XVI. **The Same,** vol. iii (1558–75). Edited by the Right Rev. W. H. FRERE, D.D. Price 30s. [*Out of print.*]

XVII. **Traditional Ceremonial and Customs connected with the Scottish Liturgy.** By F. C. EELES, F.R.Hist.S., F.S.A.Scot. Price £1.

XVIII. **The Rationale of Ceremonial,** 1540–3, with Notes and Appendices and an Essay on the Regulation of Ceremonial during the Reign of King Henry VIII. By Sir C. S. COBB, K.B.E., M.V.O. Price 10s. [*Out of print.*]

XIX. **Illustrations of the Liturgy.** Thirteen drawings of the Celebration of the Holy Communion in a parish church. By CLEMENT O. SKILBECK. With Notes descriptive and explanatory, an Introduction on ' The Present Opportunity ', and a Preface on the English and American Uses. By the Rev. PERCY DEARMER, D.D. Price 4s. 6d. [*Out of print.*]

XX. **The Edwardian Inventories for the City and County of Exeter.** Edited by Miss B. CRESSWELL, from transcripts of the original documents in the Guildhall, Exeter. Price 10s.

XXI. **The Sacrament Reserved : being a History of the Practice of Reserving the Eucharist up to the IVth Lateran Council.** By the Rev. W. H. FREESTONE. Price £1.

XXII. **The Ornaments of the Ministers as shown on English Monumental Brasses.** Illustrated. By the Rev. H. J. CLAYTON, A.K.C. Price £1 5s.

XXIII. **The Chantry Certificates for Oxfordshire.** Edited and transcribed by ROSE GRAHAM, F.R.Hist.S., formerly of Somerville College, Oxford, and **The Edwardian Inventories of Church Goods for Oxfordshire.** Edited by ROSE GRAHAM from transcripts by T. CRAIB, of H.M. Public Record Office. Price 10s. 6d. [*Out of print.*]

XXIV. **Illustrations of the Occasional Offices of the Church.** Taken from Medieval pictures and miniatures. Edited by H. S. KINGSFORD, M.A. Price £1 5s.

XXV–XXVII. **Elizabethan Episcopal Administration.** An Essay introductory to a further Collection of Visitation Articles, by Professor W. M. KENNEDY, Litt.D. Vol. i: The Essay. Vol. ii: Articles, &c., 1575–83. Vol. iii: Articles, &c., 1583–1603. Price £3 3s. the set. Vol. i: The Essay, can be bought separately. Price £1 5s.

XXVIII. **Studies in the Early Roman Liturgy.** I. The Kalendar. By the Right Rev. Walter Howard Frere, D.D. Price £1 1s.

TRACTS

PRAYER BOOK REVISION PAMPHLETS

PUBLISHER.—Mr. Humphrey Milford, Oxford University Press, Amen House, Warwick Square, London, E.C. 4.

PRINTED IN GREAT BRITAIN AT THE UNIVERSITY PRESS, OXFORD
BY JOHN JOHNSON, PRINTER TO THE UNIVERSITY